Collins

Spanish

Vocabulary

HarperCollins Publishers
Westerhill Road
Bishopbriggs
Glasgow
G64 2QT
Great Britain

Second Edition 2012

Reprint 10 9 8 7 6 5 4 3 2 1 0

© HarperCollins Publishers 2006, 2012

ISBN 978-0-00-748393-8

Collins® is a registered trademark of
HarperCollins Publishers Limited

www.collinslanguage.com

A catalogue record for this book is available
from the British Library

Typeset by Davidson Publishing Solutions,
Glasgow

Printed in Great Britain by Clays Ltd, St Ives plc

Acknowledgements
We would like to thank those authors and
publishers who kindly gave permission for
copyright material to be used in the Collins
Word Web. We would also like to thank
Times Newspapers Ltd for providing
valuable data.

EDITOR
Persephone Lock

CONTRIBUTORS
Phyllis Buchanan
José Martín Galera
Val McNulty
Julie Muleba
Victoria Romero Cerro

FOR THE PUBLISHER
Lucy Cooper
Elaine Higgleton
Susanne Reichert
Lisa Sutherland

William Collins' dream of knowledge for all began with the publication of his first book in 1819. A self-educated mill worker, he not only enriched millions of lives, but also founded a flourishing publishing house. Today, staying true to this spirit, Collins books are packed with inspiration, innovation, and practical expertise. They place you at the centre of a world of possibility and give you exactly what you need to explore it.

Language is the key to this exploration, and at the heart of Collins Dictionaries is language as it is really used. New words, phrases, and meanings spring up every day, and all of them are captured and analysed by the Collins Word Web. Constantly updated, and with over 4.5 billion entries, this living language resource is unique to our dictionaries.

Words are tools for life. And a Collins Dictionary makes them work for you.

Collins. Do more.

contents

air travel	10
animals	14
bikes	18
birds	20
body	22
calendar	26
camping	30
careers	32
cars	38
clothes	44
colours	48
computing and IT	50
countries and nationalities	52
countryside	58
describing people	62
education	66
environment	74
family	78
farm	82
fish and insects	86
food and drink	88
free time	96
fruit	100
furniture and appliances	102
geographical names	106
greetings and everyday phrases	108
health	112
hotel	116
house – general	120
house – particular	124
information and services	128
law	134
materials	138
music	142
numbers and quantities	144
personal items	150
plants and gardens	152
seaside and boats	156
shopping	160

6 contents

sports   166
theatre and cinema   170
time   174
tools   178
town   180
trains   186
trees   190
vegetables   192
vehicles   194
the weather   198
youth hostelling   202

supplementary vocabulary
  articles and pronouns   204
  conjunctions   206
  adjectives   207
  adverbs and prepositions   215
  nouns   220
  verbs   231

English index   243

The *Easy Learning Spanish Vocabulary* is designed for both young and adult learners. Whether you are starting to learn Spanish for the first time, revising for school exams or simply want to brush up on your Spanish, the *Easy Learning Spanish Vocabulary* offers you the information you require in a clear and accessible format.

This book is divided into 50 topics, arranged in alphabetical order. This thematic approach enables you to learn related words and phrases together, so that you can become confident in using particular vocabulary in context.

Vocabulary within each topic is divided into nouns and useful phrases which are aimed at helping you to express yourself in idiomatic Spanish. Vocabulary within each topic is graded to help you prioritize your learning. Essential words include the basic words you will need to be able to communicate effectively, important words help expand your knowledge, and useful words provide additional vocabulary which will enable you to express yourself more fully.

Nouns are grouped by gender: masculine ("el") nouns are given on the left-hand page, and feminine ("la") nouns on the right-hand page, enabling you to memorize words according to their gender. In addition, all feminine forms of adjectives are shown, as are irregular plurals.

At the end of the book you will find a list of supplementary vocabulary, grouped according to part of speech – adjective, verb, noun and so on. This is vocabulary which you will come across in many everyday situations.

Finally, there is an English index which lists all the essential and important nouns given under the topic headings for quick reference.

The *Easy Learning Spanish Vocabulary* helps you to consolidate your language learning. Together with the other titles in the *Easy Learning* range you can be sure that you have all the help you need when learning Spanish at your fingertips.

ABBREVIATIONS

adj	adjective
adv	adverb
algn	alguien
conj	conjunction
f	feminine
inv	invariable
LAm	word used in Latin America
m	masculine
m+f	masculine and feminine form
Mex	word used in Mexico
n	noun
pl	plural
prep	preposition
sb	somebody
sing	singular
Sp	word used in Spain
sth	something

The swung dash ~ is used to indicate the basic elements of the compound and appropriate endings are then added.

PLURALS AND GENDER

In Spanish, if a noun ends in a vowel it generally takes –s in the plural (casa > casas). If it ends in a consonant (including y) it generally takes –es in the plural (reloj > relojes). If it doesn't follow these rules, then the plural will be given in the text.

Although most masculine nouns take "el" and most feminine nouns take "la", you will find a few nouns grouped under feminine words which take "el" (el agua water; el arca chest; el aula classroom) because they are actually feminine.

ESSENTIAL WORDS *(masculine)*

el	**aeropuerto**	airport
el	**agente de viajes**	travel agent
el	**alquiler de coches**	car hire
el	**avión** (*pl* aviones)	plane
el	**billete** (*Sp*), el **boleto** (*LAm*)	ticket
el	**bolso**	bag
el	**carnet** (*or* carné) **de identidad**	ID card
	(*pl* carnets *or* carnés ~ ~)	
el	**enlace**	connection
el	**equipaje**	luggage
el	**equipaje de mano**	hand luggage
el	**horario**	timetable
el	**número**	number
el	**oficial de aduanas**	customs officer
el	**pasajero**	passenger
el	**pasaporte**	passport
el	**(precio del) billete** (*Sp*) *or* **boleto** (*LAm*)	fare
el	**retraso**	delay
los	**servicios**	toilets
el	**taxi**	taxi
el	**turista**	tourist
el	**viaje**	trip
el	**viajero**	traveller

USEFUL PHRASES

viajar en avión to travel by plane

un billete (*Sp*) *or* **boleto** (*LAm*) **de ida** a single ticket

un billete (*Sp*) *or* **boleto** (*LAm*) **de ida y vuelta, un boleto redondo** (*Mex*)
  a return ticket

reservar un billete (*Sp*) *or* **boleto** (*LAm*) **de avión** to book a plane ticket

"por avión" "by airmail"

facturar el equipaje to check in one's luggage

perdí el enlace I missed my connection

el avión ha despegado/ha aterrizado the plane has taken off/has landed

el panel de llegadas/salidas the arrivals/departures board

el vuelo número 776 procedente de Madrid/con destino Madrid flight
  number 776 from Madrid/to Madrid

ESSENTIAL WORDS *(feminine)*

la **aduana**	customs
la **agente de viajes**	travel agent
la **cancelación** (*pl* cancelaciones)	cancellation
la **duty free**	duty-free (shop)
la **entrada**	entrance
la **información** (*pl* informaciones)	information desk; information
la **llegada**	arrival
la **maleta**	bag; suitcase
la **oficial de aduanas**	customs officer
la **pasajera**	passenger
la **puerta de embarque**	departure gate
la **reserva**	reservation
la **salida**	departure; exit
la **salida de emergencia**	emergency exit
la **tarifa**	fare
la **tarjeta de embarque**	boarding card
la **turista**	tourist
la **viajera**	traveller

USEFUL PHRASES

recoger el equipaje to collect one's luggage
"recogida de equipajes" "baggage reclaim"
pasar por la aduana to go through customs
tengo algo que declarar I have something to declare
no tengo nada que declarar I have nothing to declare
registrar el equipaje to search the luggage

IMPORTANT WORDS *(masculine)*

el	**accidente de avión**	plane crash
el	**billete electrónico**	e-ticket
el	**carrito**	trolley
el	**cinturón de seguridad**	seat belt
	(pl cinturones ~~)	
el	**helicóptero**	helicopter
el	**mapa**	map
el	**mareo (en avión)**	airsickness
el	**piloto**	pilot
el	**reloj**	clock
el	**vuelo**	flight

USEFUL WORDS *(masculine)*

el	**asiento**	seat
el	**aterrizaje**	landing
el	**auxiliar de vuelo**	steward; flight attendant
el	**cambiador para bebés**	mother and baby room
el	**control de seguridad**	security check
el	**controlador aéreo**	air-traffic controller
los	**derechos de aduana**	customs duty
el	**despegue**	take-off
el	**detector de metales**	metal detector
el	**embarque**	boarding
el	**horario**	timetable
el	**jumbo**	jumbo jet
los	**mandos**	controls
el	**paracaídas** *(pl inv)*	parachute
el	**radar**	radar
el	**reactor**	jet plane/engine
el	**satélite**	satellite terminal
el	**veraneante**	holiday-maker

USEFUL PHRASES

a bordo on board; **"prohibido fumar"** "no smoking"
"abróchense el cinturón de seguridad" "fasten your seat belts"
estamos sobrevolando Londres we are flying over London
me estoy mareando I am feeling sick; **secuestrar un avión** to hijack a plane

IMPORTANT WORDS *(feminine)*

la	**duración** *(pl* duraciones)	length; duration
la	**escalera mecánica**	escalator
la	**piloto**	pilot
la	**sala de embarque**	departure lounge
la	**velocidad**	speed

USEFUL WORDS *(feminine)*

el	**ala** *(pl f* las alas)	wing
la	**altitud**	altitude
la	**altura**	height
la	**auxiliar de vuelo**	air hostess; flight attendant
la	**barrera del sonido**	sound barrier
la	**bolsa de aire**	air pocket
la	**caja negra**	black box
la	**cinta transportadora**	carousel
la	**controladora aérea**	air-traffic controller
la	**escala**	stopover
la	**etiqueta**	label
la	**hélice**	propeller
la	**línea aérea**	airline
la	**pista (de aterrizaje)**	runway
la	**terminal**	terminal
la	**tienda libre de impuestos**	duty-free shop
la	**torre de control**	control tower
la	**tripulación** *(pl* tripulaciones)	crew
la	**turbulencia**	turbulence
la	**ventanilla**	window
la	**veraneante**	holiday-maker

USEFUL PHRASES

"pasajeros del vuelo AB251 con destino Madrid embarquen por la puerta 51" "flight AB251 to Madrid now boarding at gate 51"

hicimos escala en Nueva York we stopped over in New York

un aterrizaje forzoso *or* **de emergencia** an emergency landing

un aterrizaje violento a crash landing

cigarrillos libres de impuestos duty-free cigarettes

ESSENTIAL WORDS *(masculine)*

el	**animal**	animal
el	**buey** *(pl ~es)*	ox
el	**caballo**	horse
el	**cachorro**	puppy
el	**cerdo**	pig
el	**conejo**	rabbit
el	**cordero**	lamb
el	**elefante**	elephant
el	**gato**	cat
el	**gatito**	kitten
el	**hámster** *(pl ~s)*	hamster
el	**león** *(pl leones)*	lion
el	**pájaro**	bird
el	**perro**	dog
el	**perrito**	puppy
el	**pelaje**	fur, coat
el	**pelo**	coat, hair
el	**pescado**	fish
el	**pez** *(pl peces)*	fish
el	**potro**	foal
el	**ratón** *(pl ratones)*	mouse
el	**ternero**	calf
el	**tigre**	tiger
el	**zoo** *(pl ~s)*	zoo
el	**zoológico**	zoo

USEFUL PHRASES

me gustan los gatos, odio las serpientes, prefiero los ratones I like cats, I hate snakes, I prefer mice

tenemos 12 animales en casa we have 12 pets in our house

no tenemos animales en casa we have no pets in our house

los animales salvajes wild animals

los animales domésticos *or* **las mascotas** pets

el ganado livestock

meter un animal en una jaula to put an animal in a cage

liberar un animal to set an animal free

ESSENTIAL WORDS *(feminine)*

el	**ave** *(pl f* las aves)	bird
la	**gata**	cat *(female)*
la	**oveja**	ewe
la	**perra**	dog *(female)*
la	**tortuga**	tortoise
la	**vaca**	cow

IMPORTANT WORDS *(feminine)*

la	**cola**	tail
la	**jaula**	cage

USEFUL PHRASES

el perro ladra the dog barks; **gruñe** it growls
el gato maulla the cat miaows; **ronronea** it purrs
me gusta la equitación *or* **montar a caballo** I like horse-riding
a caballo on horseback
"cuidado con el perro" "beware of the dog"
"no se admiten perros" "no dogs allowed"
"¡quieto!" *(to dog)* "down!"
los derechos de los animales animal rights

USEFUL WORDS *(masculine)*

el	**asno**	donkey
el	**burro**	donkey
el	**camello**	camel
el	**canguro**	kangaroo
el	**caparazón** *(pl* caparazones)	shell *(of tortoise)*
el	**casco**	hoof
el	**cerdo**	pig
el	**ciervo**	stag
el	**cocodrilo**	crocodile
el	**colmillo**	tusk
el	**conejillo de Indias**	guinea pig
el	**cuerno**	horn
el	**erizo**	hedgehog
el	**hipopótamo**	hippopotamus
el	**hocico**	snout
el	**lobo**	wolf
el	**macho cabrío**	billy goat
el	**mono**	monkey
el	**mulo**	mule
el	**murciélago**	bat
el	**oso**	bear
el	**oso polar**	polar bear
el	**pavo**	turkey
el	**pony** *(pl* ~s)	pony
el	**rinoceronte**	rhinoceros
el	**sapo**	toad
el	**tiburón** *(pl* tiburones)	shark
el	**topo**	mole
el	**toro**	bull
el	**zorro**	fox

ESSENTIAL WORDS *(feminine)*

la	**bici**	bike
la	**bicicleta**	bicycle
la	**bicicleta de montaña**	mountain bike
la	**vuelta ciclista a España**	Tour of Spain

IMPORTANT WORDS *(feminine)*

la	**rueda**	wheel
la	**velocidad**	speed; gear

USEFUL WORDS *(feminine)*

la	**alforja**	pannier
la	**barra**	crossbar
la	**bomba**	pump
la	**cadena**	chain
la	**cuesta**	slope
la	**cumbre**	top *(of hill)*
la	**dínamo**	dynamo
la	**luz delantera** *(pl luces ~s)*	front light
la	**pendiente**	slope
la	**salpicadera** *(Mex)*	mudguard
la	**subida**	climb
la	**válvula**	valve

USEFUL PHRASES

dar una vuelta *or* **pasear en bici(cleta)** to go for a bike ride
tener un pinchazo *or* **una rueda pinchada** to have a puncture
arreglar un pinchazo to mend a puncture
la rueda delantera/trasera the front/back wheel
inflar las ruedas to blow up the tyres
brillante, reluciente shiny
oxidado(a) rusty
fluorescente fluorescent

ESSENTIAL WORDS *(masculine)*

el	**cielo**	sky
el	**gallo**	cock
el	**ganso**	goose
el	**loro**	parrot
el	**pájaro**	bird
el	**pato**	duck
el	**pavo**	turkey
el	**periquito**	budgie

USEFUL WORDS *(masculine)*

el	**avestruz** *(pl* avestruces)	ostrich
el	**búho**	owl
el	**buitre**	vulture
el	**canario**	canary
el	**chochín** *(pl* chochines)	wren
el	**cisne**	swan
el	**cuervo**	raven; crow
el	**cuco**	cuckoo
el	**estornino**	starling
el	**faisán** *(pl* faisanes)	pheasant
el	**gorrión** *(pl* gorriones)	sparrow
el	**halcón** *(pl* halcones)	falcon
el	**herrerillo**	bluetit
el	**huevo**	egg
el	**martín pescador**	kingfisher
	(pl martines ~es)	
el	**mirlo**	blackbird
el	**nido**	nest
el	**pájaro carpintero**	woodpecker
el	**pavo real**	peacock
el	**petirrojo**	robin
el	**pico**	beak
el	**pingüino**	penguin
el	**ruiseñor**	nightingale
el	**tordo**	thrush
el	**urogallo**	grouse

ESSENTIAL WORDS (*feminine*)

la **gallina** — hen

USEFUL WORDS (*feminine*)

el **águila** (*pl f* las águilas)	eagle
el **ala** (*pl f* las alas)	wing
la **alondra**	lark
el **ave** (*pl f* las aves)	bird
el **ave de rapiña** (*pl f* las ~s ~~)	bird of prey
el **ave rapaz** (*pl f* las ~s rapaces)	bird of prey
la **cigüeña**	stork
la **codorniz** (*pl* codornices)	quail
la **gaviota**	seagull
la **golondrina**	swallow
la **grajilla**	jackdaw
la **jaula**	cage
la **paloma**	pigeon; dove
la **perdiz** (*pl* perdices)	partridge
la **pluma**	feather
la **urraca**	magpie

USEFUL PHRASES

volar to fly
emprender vuelo to fly away
construir un nido to build a nest
silbar to whistle
cantar to sing
la gente los mete en jaulas people put them in cages
hibernar to hibernate
poner un huevo to lay an egg
un ave migratoria a migratory bird

ESSENTIAL WORDS (*masculine*)

el	**brazo**	arm
el	**cabello**	hair
el	**corazón** (*pl* corazones)	heart
el	**cuerpo**	body
el	**dedo**	finger
el	**diente**	tooth
el	**estómago**	stomach
el	**ojo**	eye
el	**pelo**	hair
el	**pie**	foot
el	**rostro**	face

IMPORTANT WORDS (*masculine*)

el	**cuello**	neck
el	**hombro**	shoulder
el	**pecho**	chest; bust
el	**pulgar**	thumb
el	**tobillo**	ankle

USEFUL PHRASES
de pie standing
sentado(a) sitting
tumbado(a) lying

ESSENTIAL WORDS *(feminine)*

la	**boca**	mouth
la	**cabeza**	head
la	**espalda**	back
la	**garganta**	throat
la	**mano**	hand
la	**nariz** *(pl narices)*	nose
la	**oreja**	ear
la	**pierna**	leg
la	**rodilla**	knee

IMPORTANT WORDS *(feminine)*

la	**barbilla**	chin
la	**cara**	face
la	**ceja**	eyebrow
la	**frente**	forehead
la	**lengua**	tongue
la	**mejilla**	cheek
la	**piel**	skin
la	**sangre**	blood
la	**voz** *(pl voces)*	voice

USEFUL PHRASES

grande big
alto(a) tall
pequeño(a) small
bajo(a) short
gordo(a) fat
flaco(a) skinny
delgado(a) slim
bonito(a) pretty
feo(a) ugly

USEFUL WORDS *(masculine)*

el	**cerebro**	brain
el	**codo**	elbow
el	**cutis** *(pl inv)*	skin, complexion
el	**dedo del pie**	toe
el	**dedo índice**	forefinger
el	**dedo gordo**	the big toe
los	**dedos del pie**	toes
el	**esqueleto**	skeleton
el	**gesto**	gesture
el	**hígado**	liver
el	**hueso**	bone
el	**labio**	lip
el	**músculo**	muscle
el	**muslo**	thigh
el	**párpado**	eyelid
el	**pulmón** *(pl pulmones)*	lung
el	**puño**	fist
el	**rasgo**	feature
el	**riñón** *(pl riñones)*	kidney
el	**seno**	breast
el	**talle**	waist
el	**talón** *(pl talones)*	heel
el	**trasero**	bottom

USEFUL PHRASES

sonarse (la nariz) to blow one's nose
cortarse las uñas to cut one's nails
cortarse el pelo to have one's hair cut
encogerse de hombros to shrug one's shoulders
asentir/decir que sí con la cabeza to nod one's head
negar/decir que no con la cabeza to shake one's head
ver to see; **oír** to hear; **sentir** to feel
oler to smell; **tocar** to touch; **probar** to taste
estrechar la mano a alguien to shake hands with somebody
saludar a alguien con la mano to wave at somebody
señalar algo to point at something

USEFUL WORDS *(feminine)*

la	**arteria**	artery
la	**cadera**	hip
la	**carne**	flesh
la	**columna (vertebral)**	spine
la	**costilla**	rib
la	**facción** (*pl* facciones)	feature
la	**mandíbula**	jaw
la	**muñeca**	wrist
la	**nuca**	nape of the neck
la	**pantorrilla**	calf (*of leg*)
la	**pestaña**	eyelash
la	**planta del pie**	sole of the foot
la	**pupila**	pupil (*of the eye*)
la	**sien**	temple (*of head*)
la	**talla**	size
la	**tez** (*pl* teces)	complexion
la	**uña**	nail
la	**vena**	vein

USEFUL PHRASES

contorno de caderas hip measurement
cintura waist measurement
contorno de pecho chest measurement
sordo(a) deaf
ciego(a) blind
mudo(a) mute
discapacitado(a) disabled
disminuido(a) psíquico(a) person with learning difficulties
él es más alto que tú he is taller than you
ella ha crecido mucho she has grown a lot
estoy demasiado gordo(a) *or* **tengo sobrepeso** I am overweight
ella ha engordado/adelgazado she has put on/lost weight
ella mide 1,47 metros she is 1.47 metres tall
él pesa 40 kilos he weighs 40 kilos

SEASONS

la	**primavera**	spring
el	**verano**	summer
el	**otoño**	autumn
el	**invierno**	winter

MONTHS

enero	January	**julio**	July
febrero	February	**agosto**	August
marzo	March	**septiembre**	September
abril	April	**octubre**	October
mayo	May	**noviembre**	November
junio	June	**diciembre**	December

DAYS OF THE WEEK

lunes	Monday
martes	Tuesday
miércoles	Wednesday
jueves	Thursday
viernes	Friday
sábado	Saturday
domingo	Sunday

USEFUL PHRASES
en primavera/verano/otoño/invierno in
   spring/summer/autumn/winter
en mayo in May
el 10 de julio de 2006 on 10 July 2006
es 3 de diciembre it's 3rd December
los sábados voy a la piscina on Saturdays I go to the swimming pool
el sábado fui a la piscina on Saturday I went to the swimming pool
el próximo sábado/el sábado pasado next/last Saturday
el sábado anterior/siguiente the previous/following Saturday

CALENDAR

el	**calendario**	calendar
el	**día**	day
los	**días de la semana**	days of the week
el	**día festivo**	public holiday
la	**estación** (*pl* estaciones)	season
el	**mes**	month
la	**semana**	week

USEFUL PHRASES

el día de los (Santos) Inocentes April Fools' Day (*celebrated on 28 December in Spain*)

la broma del día de los (Santos) Inocentes April fool's trick

el primero de mayo May Day

el día de la Hispanidad Columbus Day (*Spain's national day, celebrated on 12 October*)

el himno nacional de España Spain's national anthem

el día D D-Day

el día de San Valentín St Valentine's Day

el día de Todos los Santos All Saints' Day

la Semana Santa Easter

el Domingo de Resurrección *or* **Pascua** Easter Sunday

el Lunes de Pascua Easter Monday

el Miércoles de Ceniza Ash Wednesday

el Viernes Santo Good Friday

la Cuaresma Lent

la Pascua judía Passover

el Ramadán Ramadan

el Hanukkah Hanukkah *or* Hanukah

el Divali *or* **el Festival de la Luz** Divali *or* Diwali

el Adviento Advent

la Nochebuena Christmas Eve

la Navidad Christmas

en Navidad at Christmas

el día de Navidad Christmas Day

la Nochevieja New Year's Eve

el día de Año Nuevo New Year's Day

la cena *or* **fiesta de Fin de Año** New Year's Eve dinner *or* party

ESSENTIAL WORDS *(masculine)*

el	**aniversario de boda**	wedding anniversary
el	**cumpleaños** *(pl inv)*	birthday
el	**(día del) santo**	saint's day
el	**divorcio**	divorce
el	**matrimonio**	marriage
el	**regalo**	present

IMPORTANT WORDS *(masculine)*

el	**compromiso**	engagement
el	**festival**	festival
los	**fuegos artificiales**	fireworks; firework display
el	**nacimiento**	birth
el	**parque de atracciones**	fun fair

USEFUL WORDS *(masculine)*

el	**bautismo**	christening
el	**cementerio**	cemetery
el	**entierro**	funeral
el	**festival folclórico**	folk festival
el	**testigo**	witness
el	**regalo de Navidad**	Christmas present

USEFUL PHRASES

celebrar el cumpleaños to celebrate one's birthday
mi hermana nació en 1995 my sister was born in 1995
ella acaba de cumplir 17 años she's just turned 17
él me dio este regalo he gave me this present
¡te lo regalo! I'm giving it to you!
gracias thank you
divorciarse to get divorced
casarse to get married
comprometerse (con algn) to get engaged (to sb)
mi padre murió hace dos años my father died two years ago
enterrar to bury

ESSENTIAL WORDS *(feminine)*

la	**boda**	wedding
la	**cita**	appointment, date
la	**fecha**	date
la	**fiesta**	festival; fair; party

IMPORTANT WORDS *(feminine)*

las	**fiestas**	festivities
la	**feria**	fair
la	**muerte**	death
la	**hoguera**	bonfire

USEFUL WORDS *(feminine)*

la	**ceremonia**	ceremony
la	**dama de honor**	bridesmaid
la	**invitación de boda**	wedding invitation
	(*pl* invitaciones ~~)	
la	**jubilación** (*pl* jubilaciones)	retirement
la	**luna de miel**	honeymoon
la	**procesión** (*pl* procesiones)	procession; march
la	**tarjeta de felicitación**	greetings card
la	**testigo**	witness

USEFUL PHRASES

bodas de plata/oro/diamante silver/golden/diamond wedding anniversary
desear a algn (un) Feliz Año to wish sb a happy New Year
dar *or* **hacer una fiesta** to have a party
invitar a los amigos to invite one's friends
elegir un regalo to choose a gift
¡Feliz navidad! *or* **¡Felices Pascuas!** Happy Christmas!
¡Feliz cumpleaños! happy birthday!
(con) nuestros mejores deseos best wishes

ESSENTIAL WORDS *(masculine)*

los	**aseos**	toilets
los	**baños** *(LAm)*	washrooms; toilets
el	**bote**	tin, can
el	**camping** *(pl ~s)*	camping; campsite
el	**campista**	camper
el	**cerillo** *(LAm)*	match
el	**cubo de la basura**	dustbin
el	**cuchillo**	knife
el	**depósito de butano**	butane store
el	**emplazamiento**	pitch, site
el	**espejo**	mirror
el	**gas**	gas
el	**guarda**	warden
el	**lavabo**	washbasin
el	**plato**	plate
los	**servicios** *(Sp)*	washrooms; toilets
el	**suplemento**	extra charge
el	**tenedor**	fork
el	**trailer** *(pl ~s) (LAm)*	trailer
el	**vehículo**	vehicle

IMPORTANT WORDS *(masculine)*

el	**abrelatas** *(pl inv)*	tin-opener
el	**colchón inflable** *(pl colchones ~s)*	airbed
el	**detergente**	washing powder
el	**enchufe**	socket
el	**hornillo**	stove
el	**sacacorchos** *(pl inv)*	corkscrew
el	**saco de dormir**	sleeping bag

USEFUL PHRASES

ir de *or* **hacer camping** to go camping
acampar to camp
bien equipado(a) well equipped
hacer una hoguera to make a fire

ESSENTIAL WORDS *(feminine)*

el	**agua (no) potable** *(f)*	(non-)drinking water
la	**alberca** *(Mex)*	swimming pool
la	**caja**	box
la	**cama plegable**	camp bed
la	**campista**	camper
la	**caravana**	caravan; motorhome
la	**carpa** *(LAm)*	tent
la	**cerilla**	match
la	**comida enlatada**	tinned food
la	**cuchara**	spoon
la	**ducha**	shower
la	**hoguera de campamento**	campfire
la	**lata**	tin, can
la	**lavadora**	washing machine
la	**linterna**	torch
la	**mesa**	table
la	**navaja**	penknife
la	**noche**	night
la	**piscina** *(Sp)*	swimming pool
la	**sala**	room; hall
la	**tienda (de campaña)** *(Sp)*	tent
la	**tumbona**	deckchair

IMPORTANT WORDS *(feminine)*

la	**barbacoa**	barbecue
la	**colada**	washing
las	**instalaciones sanitarias**	washing facilities
la	**lavandería**	launderette
la	**mochila**	rucksack
las	**normas**	rules
la	**sala de juegos**	games room
la	**sombra**	shade; shadow
la	**toma de corriente**	socket

USEFUL PHRASES
montar una tienda to pitch a tent
asar unas salchichas (a la parrilla) to grill some sausages

ESSENTIAL WORDS *(masculine)*

el	**aeromozo** *(LAm)*	steward; flight attendant
el	**agricultor**	farmer
el	**auxiliar de vuelo** *(Sp)*	steward; flight attendant
el	**banco**	bank
el	**bombero**	fireman
el	**cajero**	check-out assistant
el	**cartero**	postman
el	**diseñador de páginas web**	web designer
el	**electricista**	electrician
el	**empleado**	employee
el	**empresario**	employer
el	**enfermero**	nurse
el	**farmacéutico**	chemist
el	**informático**	computer programmer
el	**jefe**	boss
el	**maquinista**	engineer; train driver
el	**mecánico**	mechanic
el	**médico**	doctor
el	**minero**	miner
el	**oficio**	trade
el	**orientador profesional**	careers adviser
el	**policía**	policeman
el	**profesor**	teacher
el	**propietario de un taller** (mecánico *or* de reparaciones)	garage owner
el	**redactor**	editor
el	**soldado**	soldier
el	**sueldo**	wages
el	**taxista**	taxi driver
el	**trabajo**	job; work
el	**vendedor**	sales assistant, shop assistant

USEFUL PHRASES

interesante/poco interesante interesting/not very interesting
él es cartero he is a postman; **él/ella es médico** he/she is a doctor
trabajar to work
hacerse, volverse to become

ESSENTIAL WORDS *(feminine)*

la **aeromoza** *(LAm)*	stewardess; flight attendant
la **agricultora**	farmer
la **ambición** *(pl ambiciones)*	ambition
la **auxiliar de vuelo**	stewardess; flight attendant
la **cajera**	check-out assistant
la **cartera**	postwoman
la **consejera profesional**	careers adviser
la **empleada**	employee
la **enfermera**	nurse
la **estrella** *(m+f)*	star
la **fábrica**	factory
la **informática**	computer programmer
la **jefa**	boss
la **jubilación** *(pl jubilaciones)*	retirement
la **mecanógrafa**	typist
la **médico**	doctor
la **oficina**	office
la **profesión** *(pl profesiones)*	profession
la **profesora**	teacher
la **recepcionista**	receptionist
la **redactora**	editor
la **secretaria**	secretary
la **vendedora**	sales assistant, shop assistant
la **vida**	life
la **vida laboral**	working life

USEFUL PHRASES

trabajar para ganarse la vida to work for one's living
mi ambición es ser juez(a) it is my ambition to be a judge
¿en qué trabajas? what do you do (for a living)?
solicitar un trabajo to apply for a job

IMPORTANT WORDS (*masculine*)

el	**aprendizaje**	apprenticeship
el	**asalariado**	wage-earner
el	**aumento**	rise
el	**autor**	author
el	**bombero**	fireman
el	**colega**	colleague
el	**comerciante**	shopkeeper
el	**contrato**	contract
el	**conserje**	caretaker
el	**decorador**	decorator
el	**desempleado**	unemployed person
el	**desempleo**	unemployment
el	**empleo**	job; situation
el	**fontanero** (*Sp*)	plumber
el	**futuro**	future
el	**gerente**	manager
el	**hombre de negocios**	businessman
el	**INEM**	employment organization; institute of employment
el	**interino**	temp
el	**jefe**	boss
el	**mercado laboral**	job market
el	**negocio** *or* los **negocios**	business
el	**óptico**	optician
el	**peluquero**	hairdresser
el	**piloto**	pilot
el	**pintor**	painter
el	**plomero** (*Mex*)	plumber
el	**presidente**	president; chairperson
el	**sindicato**	trade union
el	**trabajador**	worker
el	**trabajo**	job

USEFUL PHRASES

estar desempleado(a) *or* **en paro** to be unemployed
despedir a algn to make sb redundant
contrato indefinido/temporal/a término fijo permanent/temporary/ fixed term contract

IMPORTANT WORDS *(feminine)*

la	**acomodadora**	usher
la	**agencia de trabajo temporal**	temping agency
la	**asalariada**	wage-earner
la	**biblioteca**	library
la	**carrera**	career
la	**carta adjunta**	covering letter
la	**cocinera**	cook
la	**colega**	colleague
la	**conserje**	caretaker
la	**entrevista (de trabajo)**	(job) interview
la	**gerente**	manager
la	**huelga**	strike
la	**interina**	temp
la	**limpiadora**	cleaner
la	**mujer de negocios**	businesswoman
la	**oficina de empleo**	job centre
la	**peluquera**	hairdresser
la	**pintora**	painter
la	**política**	politics
la	**presidenta**	president; chairperson
la	**solicitud**	application
la	**trabajadora**	worker

USEFUL PHRASES

"demandas de empleo" "situations wanted"
"ofertas de empleo" "situations vacant"
estar en/pertenercer a un sindicato to be in a union
ganar 150 libras a la semana to earn £150 a week
una subida *or* **un aumento de sueldo** a pay rise
ponerse *or* **declararse en huelga** to go on strike
estar en huelga to be on strike
trabajar jornada completa/media jornada to work full-time/part-time
trabajar horas extra(s) to work overtime
reducción de la jornada laboral reduction in working hours

USEFUL WORDS *(masculine)*

el	**abogado**	lawyer
el	**agente comercial**	sales rep
el	**albañil**	mason
el	**arquitecto**	architect
el	**artista**	artist
el	**carpintero**	joiner
el	**cirujano**	surgeon
el	**contable** *(Sp)*, el **contador** *(LAm)*	accountant
el	**cosmonauta**	cosmonaut
el	**cura**	priest
el	**curso de formación**	training course
el	**diputado**	MP
el	**diseñador**	fashion designer
el	**ejecutivo**	executive
el	**escritor**	writer
el	**fotógrafo**	photographer
el	**funcionario**	civil servant
el	**horario**	schedule
el	**ingeniero**	engineer
el	**intérprete**	interpreter
el	**investigador**	researcher
el	**juez** *(pl* jueces*)*	judge
el	**marinero**	sailor
el	**modelo**	model *(person)*
el	**monitor de actividades**	activity leader
el	**negocio**	business
el	**notario**	notary
el	**paro**	unemployment benefit
el	**periodista**	journalist
el	**(período de) trabajo en prácticas**	work placement
el	**personal**	staff
el	**político**	politician
el	**director ejecutivo**	managing director
el	**procurador**	solicitor
el	**representante**	rep; sales rep
el	**sacerdote**	priest
el	**traductor**	translator
el	**veterinario**	vet
el	**viticultor**	wine grower

USEFUL WORDS *(feminine)*

la	**abogada**	lawyer
la	**administración**	administration
	(*pl* administraciones)	
el	**ama de casa** (*pl f* amas ~ ~)	housewife
la	**monitora de actividades**	activity leader
la	**artista**	artist
la	**compañía**	company
la	**contable** (*Sp*), la **contadora** (*LAm*)	accountant
la	**empresa**	company
la	**formación**	training
la	**funcionaria**	civil servant
la	**huelga de celo**	work-to-rule; go-slow
la	**indemnización por desempleo**	redundancy payment
la	**intérprete**	interpreter
la	**jueza**	judge
la	**locutora**	announcer
la	**modelo**	model (*person*)
la	**modista**	dressmaker
la	**monja**	nun
la	**orientación profesional**	careers guidance
la	**periodista**	journalist
la	**policía**	policewoman
la	**religiosa**	nun
la	**representante**	rep; sales rep
la	**taquimecanógrafa**	shorthand typist
la	**traductora**	translator

USEFUL PHRASES

el trabajo temporal seasonal work
un empleo temporal/permanente a temporary/permanent job
un trabajo a tiempo parcial (*Sp*) *or* **a medio tiempo** (*LAm*) a part-time job
ser contratado(a) to be taken on; **ser despedido(a)** to be dismissed
despedir *or* **echar a algn** to give sb the sack
buscar trabajo to look for work
hacer un curso de formación profesional to go on a training course
fichar al entrar a/al salir de trabajar to clock in/out
trabajar en horario flexible to work flexitime

ESSENTIAL WORDS (*masculine*)

el	**aceite**	oil
el	**agente de policía**	policeman
el	**aparcamiento** (*Sp*)	car park
el	**atasco**	traffic jam
el	**autoestop**	hitch-hiking
el	**autoestopista**	hitch-hiker
el	**automóvil**	car
el	**aventón** (*Mex*)	hitch-hiking
el	**callejero**	street map
el	**camión** (*pl* camiones)	lorry, truck
el	**carnet** *or* **carné de conducir**	driving licence
	(*Sp*) (*pl* ~s *or* ~s ~~)	
el	**carro** (*LAm*)	car
el	**chófer**	driver; chauffeur
el	**ciclista**	cyclist
el	**coche** (*Sp*)	car
el	**conductor**	driver
el	**cruce**	crossroads
el	**diesel**	diesel
el	**estacionamiento** (*LAm*)	car park
los	**faros**	headlights
el	**freno**	brake
el	**garaje**	garage
el	**gasoil**	diesel (*oil*)
el	**kilómetro**	kilometre
el	**litro**	litre
el	**mapa de carreteras**	road map
el	**mecánico**	mechanic
el	**neumático**	tyre
el	**número**	number
el	**parking** (*pl* ~s)	car park
el	**peaje**	toll
el	**peatón** (*pl* peatones)	pedestrian
el	**radar**	speed camera
el	**semáforo**	traffic lights
el	**trailer** (*pl* ~s) (*LAm*)	caravan
el	**viaje**	journey

ESSENTIAL WORDS *(feminine)*

el	**agua** *(f)*	water
la	**autoestopista**	hitch-hiker
la	**autopista**	motorway
la	**autopista de peaje**	toll motorway
la	**caravana** *(Sp)*	caravan
la	**carretera**	road
la	**carretera nacional**	main road
la	**chófer**	driver; chauffeur
la	**ciclista**	cyclist
la	**cochera**	garage
la	**conductora**	driver
la	**desviación** *(pl* desviaciones*)*	diversion
la	**dirección** *(pl* direcciones*)*	direction
la	**dirección asistida** *(pl* direcciones ~s*)*	power steering
la	**distancia**	distance
la	**estación de servicio** *(pl* estaciones ~ ~*)*	petrol station
la	**gasolina**	petrol
la	**gasolina sin plomo**	unleaded petrol
la	**libreta de manejar** *(Mex)*	driving licence
la	**matrícula** *(Sp)*, la **placa** *(LAm)*	(car) registration document
la	**policía**	police
la	**póliza de seguros**	insurance certificate

USEFUL PHRASES

frenar bruscamente to brake suddenly

100 kilómetros por hora 100 kilometres an hour

¿tienes carné (or carnet) de conducir? do you have a driving licence?

vamos a dar una vuelta (en coche) we're going for a drive (in the car)

¡lleno, por favor!, ¡llénelo, por favor! fill her up please!

tomar la carretera a/hacia Córdoba take the road to Córdoba

es un viaje de tres horas it's a 3-hour journey

¡buen viaje! have a good journey!

¡vámonos!, ¡en marcha! let's go!

de camino vimos ... on the way we saw ...

adelantar a un coche to overtake a car

IMPORTANT WORDS (*masculine*)

el	**accidente (de carretera)**	(road) accident
el	**aparcamiento**	parking
el	**atasco**	traffic jam
el	**camionero**	lorry driver
el	**choque**	collision
el	**cinturón de seguridad**	seat belt
	(*pl* cinturones ~ ~)	
el	**claxon** (*pl* cláxones *or* ~s)	horn
el	**código de la circulación**	highway code
el	**daño**	damage
el	**embrague**	clutch
el	**encargado de una gasolinera**	petrol pump attendant
el	**faro**	headlight
el	**maletero** (*Sp*)	boot
el	**motociclista**	motorcyclist
el	**motor**	engine
el	**motorista**	motorist
los	**papeles (del coche)**	official papers
el	**pinchazo**	puncture
el	**pito**	horn
el	**salpicadero**	dashboard
el	**seguro**	insurance
el	**surtidor (de gasolina)**	petrol pump
el	**tráfico**	traffic
el	**túnel de lavado de coches**	car wash

USEFUL PHRASES

primero enciendes *or* **pones el motor en marcha** first you switch on the engine

el motor arranca *or* **se pone en marcha** the engine starts up

el coche se pone en marcha the car moves off

estamos circulando we're driving along

acelerar to accelerate; **continuar** to continue

reducir *or* **aminorar la velocidad** *or* **la marcha** to slow down

detenerse to stop; **aparcar (el coche)** to park (the car)

apagar el motor to switch off the engine

parar con el semáforo en rojo to stop at the red light

IMPORTANT WORDS (feminine)

la	**autoescuela** (Sp)	driving school
la	**avería**	breakdown
la	**batería**	battery
la	**cajuela** (Mex)	boot
la	**calle de sentido único**	one-way street
la	**carrocería**	body work
la	**colisión** (pl **colisiones**)	collision
la	**documentación (del coche)**	official papers
la	**escuela de conductores** (LAm) or **de manejo** (Mex)	driving school
la	**frontera**	border
la	**glorieta**	roundabout
la	**grúa**	breakdown van
la	**ITV (inspección técnica de vehículos)** (Sp)	MOT test
la	**marca**	make (of car)
la	**motociclista**	motorcyclist
la	**motorista**	motorist
la	**pieza de repuesto**	spare part
la	**póliza de seguros**	insurance policy
la	**prioridad**	right of way
la	**prueba del alcohol**	Breathalyser® test
la	**puerta**	(car) door
la	**rotonda**	roundabout
la	**rueda**	tyre
la	**rueda de repuesto**	spare tyre
la	**velocidad**	speed; gear
la	**zona azul**	restricted parking zone

USEFUL PHRASES

ha habido un accidente there's been an accident

hubo seis heridos en el accidente six people were injured in the accident

¿puedo ver la documentación or **los papeles del coche, por favor?** may I see your papers please?

pinchar, tener un pinchazo to have a puncture; **arreglar** to fix

averiarse or **tener una avería** to break down

me he quedado sin gasolina I've run out of petrol

USEFUL WORDS *(masculine)*

el	**acelerador**	accelerator
el	**arcén** *(pl arcenes)*	hard shoulder
el	**autolavado**	car-wash
el	**botón de arranque** *(pl botones ~ ~)*	starter
el	**capó**	bonnet
el	**carburador**	carburettor
el	**carril**	lane
el	**catalizador**	catalytic converter
el	**conductor novel**	learner driver
el	**consumo de gasolina**	petrol consumption
el	**cuentakilómetros** *(pl inv)*	speedometer
el	**desvío**	detour
el	**guardia de tráfico**	traffic warden
el	**herido**	casualty
el	**intermitente**	indicator
el	**lavacoches** *(pl inv)*	car-wash
el	**límite de velocidad**	speed limit
el	**limpiaparabrisas** *(pl inv)*	windscreen wiper
el	**parabrisas** *(pl inv)*	windscreen
el	**parachoques** *(pl inv)*	bumper
el	**parquímetro**	parking meter
el	**pedal**	pedal
el	**policía motorizado**	motorcycle policeman
el	**profesor de autoescuela**	driving instructor
el	**remolque**	trailer
el	**retrovisor**	rear-view mirror
el	**(sistema de navegación) GPS**	satellite navigation system
el	**volante**	steering wheel

USEFUL PHRASES

en la hora punta at rush hour
le pusieron una multa de 100 euros he got a 100-euro fine
¿está asegurado? are you insured?
no olviden ponerse los cinturones de seguridad don't forget to put on your seat belts
en la frontera at the border
hacer autoestop to hitch-hike

USEFUL WORDS *(feminine)*

el	**área de descanso** *(pl f las áreas ~ ~)*	lay-by
el	**área de servicio** *(pl f las áreas ~ ~)*	service area
la	**baca**	roof rack
la	**caja de cambios**	gearbox
la	**carretera de circunvalación**	ring road
la	**clase de conducir**	driving lesson
la	**curva**	bend
la	**estación de servicio** *(pl estaciones ~ ~)*	filling station
la	**gasolinera**	filling station
la	**guardia de tráfico**	traffic warden
la	**infracción de tráfico** *(pl infracciones ~ ~)*	traffic offence
la	**matrícula**	number plate
la	**mediana**	central reservation
la	**multa**	fine
la	**parada de emergencia**	emergency stop
la	**presión**	pressure
la	**señal de tráfico**	road sign
la	**vía**	way, road; lane *(on road)*
la	**vía de acceso**	slip road
la	**víctima** *(m+f)*	casualty
la	**zona urbanizada**	built-up area

USEFUL PHRASES

la rueda delantera/trasera the front/back wheel
tenemos que desviarnos we have to make a detour
una multa por exceso de velocidad a fine for speeding
contratar a un conductor to book a driver

"ceda el paso a la derecha" "give way to the right"
"circule por la derecha" "keep to the right"
"prohibido el paso" "no entry"
"prohibido aparcar" "no parking"
"obras" "roadworks"

ESSENTIAL WORDS *(masculine)*

el **abrigo**	overcoat; coat
el **anorak** (*pl inv or* ~s)	anorak
el **bañador**	swimming trunks; swimsuit
el **bolso**	bag
el **botón** (*pl* botones)	button
el **calcetín** (*pl* calcetines)	sock
los **calzoncillos**	pants; boxer shorts
los **calzones** (*LAm*)	knickers
el **camisón** (*pl* camisones)	nightdress
el **chubasquero**	raincoat
el **cuello**	collar
el **jersey** (*pl* ~s)	jumper
el **número (de pie)**	(shoe) size
el **pantalón** (*pl* pantalones)	trousers
los **(pantalones) vaqueros**	jeans
el **pañuelo**	handkerchief
el **paraguas** (*pl inv*)	umbrella
el **pijama**	pyjamas
el **sombrero**	hat
el **talle**	waist
el **traje**	suit (*for man*); costume
el **traje de chaqueta**	suit
el **vestido**	dress
el **zapato**	shoe

IMPORTANT WORDS *(masculine)*

el **bolsillo**	pocket
el **bolso**	handbag
el **cinturón** (*pl* cinturones)	belt
el **guante**	glove
el **impermeable**	raincoat
los **pantalones cortos**	shorts
el **uniforme**	uniform

ESSENTIAL WORDS *(feminine)*

la	**braga (del bikini)**	bikini bottoms
las	**bragas** *(Sp)*	pants; knickers
la	**camisa**	shirt
la	**camiseta**	T-shirt
la	**capucha**	hood
la	**chaqueta**	jacket
la	**corbata**	tie
la	**falda**	skirt
las	**medias**	tights
la	**moda**	fashion
la	**parka**	parka
la	**ropa**	clothes
la	**ropa interior**	underwear
la	**sandalia**	sandal
la	**talla**	size

IMPORTANT WORDS *(feminine)*

la	**americana**	jacket *(for man)*
la	**blusa**	blouse
la	**bota**	boot
las	**prendas de vestir**	clothes
la	**zapatilla**	slipper

USEFUL PHRASES

por la mañana me visto in the morning I get dressed
por la tarde me desvisto in the evening I get undressed
cuando llego a casa del colegio me cambio when I get home from school
  I get changed
llevar, llevar puesto to wear
ponerse to put on
eso es muy elegante that's very smart
(eso) te queda bien that suits you
¿qué talla tienes (or tiene)? what size do you take?
¿qué número de pie tienes (or tiene)? what shoe size do you take?
tengo un 38 (de pie), calzo un 38 I take size 38 in shoes

USEFUL WORDS *(masculine)*

los	**accesorios**	accessories
el	**bastón** *(pl bastones)*	walking stick
el	**bolso bandolera** *(pl ~s ~)*	shoulder bag
el	**cárdigan** *(pl ~s)*	cardigan
el	**chaleco**	vest; waistcoat
el	**chándal** *(pl ~s)*	tracksuit
los	**cordones**	(shoe)laces
el	**delantal**	apron
el	**desfile de moda**	fashion show
el	**tocado (de plumas, flores o cintas)**	fascinator
el	**foulard** *(pl ~s)*	scarf
el	**lazo**	ribbon
el	**mono**	overalls
el	**ojal**	buttonhole
los	**pantis**	tights
el	**pañuelo**	scarf
el	**peto**	overalls; dungarees
el	**polar**	fleece
el	**polo**	polo shirt
el	**probador**	fitting room
el	**sujetador**	bra
el	**traje de chaqueta**	suit *(for woman)*
el	**traje de etiqueta**	evening dress *(for man)*
el	**traje de noche**	evening dress *(for woman)*
el	**traje pantalón** *(pl ~s ~)*	trouser suit
los	**tirantes**	braces
el	**vestido de novia**	wedding dress
los	**zapatos de tacón**	high heels
los	**zapatos de tacón de aguja**	stiletto heels

USEFUL WORDS *(feminine)*

la **alpargata**	espadrille
la **alta costura**	haute couture
la **bandolera**	shoulder bag
la **bata**	dressing gown
las **bermudas**	Bermuda shorts
la **boina**	beret
la **bufanda**	scarf
la **camiseta con capucha**	hooded top
la **camiseta sin mangas**	tank top
las **chanclas**	flip flops
la **cinta**	ribbon
la **colada**	washing
la **combinación** (*pl* combinaciones)	underskirt
la **cremallera**	zip
la(s) **enagua(s)**	underskirt
la **falda pantalón** (*pl* ~s ~)	culottes
la **gorra**	cap
la **limpieza en seco**	dry-cleaning
la **manga**	sleeve
las **medias**	stockings
la **pajarita**	bow tie
la **rebeca**	cardigan
la **ropa blanca**	washing
la **sudadera**	sweatshirt
las **zapatillas de deporte**	trainers

USEFUL PHRASES

largo(a) long; **corto(a)** short
un vestido de manga corta/larga a short-sleeved/long-sleeved dress
estrecho(a), ajustado(a) tight
amplio(a), suelto(a) loose
una falda ajustada *or* **ceñida** a tight skirt
a rayas, de rayas striped; **a cuadros, de cuadros** checked; **de lunares** spotted
ropa de sport, ropa informal casual clothes
con vestido de noche in evening dress
a la moda, de moda fashionable; **moderno(a)** trendy
pasado(a) de moda, anticuado(a) old-fashioned

amarillo(a)	yellow
azul	blue
azul celeste	sky blue
azul claro	pale blue
azul marino	navy blue
azul oscuro	dark blue
azul real	royal blue
beige, beis	beige
blanco(a)	white
burdeos (*pl inv*)	maroon
crudo(a)	natural
dorado(a)	golden
granate	maroon
gris	grey
malva	mauve
marrón (*pl* marrones)	brown
morado(a)	purple
naranja	orange
negro(a)	black
rojo(a)	red
rojo fuerte *or* intenso	bright red
rosa	pink
turquesa	turquoise
verde	green
violeta	violet

USEFUL PHRASES

el color colour

¿de qué color tienes (*or* **tiene**) **los ojos/el pelo?** what colour are your eyes/ is your hair?

el azul te sienta bien blue suits you; the blue one suits you

pintar algo de azul to paint sth blue

los zapatos azules blue shoes

los zapatos azul claro light blue shoes

(ella) tiene los ojos verdes she has green eyes

cambiar de color to change colour

la Casa Blanca the White House

un (hombre) blanco a white man

una (mujer) blanca a white woman

un (hombre) negro a black man

una (mujer) negra a black woman

blanco como la nieve as white as snow

Blancanieves Snow White

Caperucita Roja Little Red Riding Hood

ponerse colorado(a) *or* **rojo(a)** to turn red

sonrojarse de vergüenza to blush with shame

blanco(a) como el papel as white as a sheet

muy moreno(a), muy bronceado(a) as brown as a berry

(él) estaba cubierto de cardenales he was black and blue

un ojo morado a black eye

un filete muy poco hecho a very rare steak, an underdone steak

ESSENTIAL WORDS (*masculine*)

el	**ordenador (personal)**	(personal) computer
el	**programa**	program
el	**programador**	programmer
el	**ratón** (*pl* ratones)	mouse

USEFUL WORDS (*masculine*)

el	**adaptador**	dongle
el	**blog** (*pl* ~s)	blog
el	**CD-ROM** (*pl inv*)	CD-ROM
el	**corrector ortográfico**	spellchecker
el	**correo electrónico**	email
el	**cursor**	cursor
los	**datos**	data
el	**disco duro**	hard disk
el	**documento**	document
el	**fichero**	file
el	**icono**	icon
el	**Internet**	internet
el	**juego de ordenador**	computer game
el	**mail** (*pl* ~s)	email
los	**medios sociales**	social media
el	**menú**	menu
el	**microblog** (*pl* ~s)	microblog
el	**módem** (*pl* ~s)	modem
el	**monitor**	monitor
el	**navegador**	browser
el	**nombre de usuario**	username
el	**ordenador portátil**	laptop
el	**pirata informático**	hacker
el	**red social**	social networking site
el	**servidor**	server
el	**sitio web**	website
el	**software** (*pl inv*)	software
el	**teclado**	keyboard
el	**virus** (*pl inv*)	virus
el	**Web** (*pl* ~s)	Web
el	**wifi**	wifi

ESSENTIAL WORDS *(feminine)*

la **impresora**	printer
la **informática**	computer science; computer studies

USEFUL WORDS *(feminine)*

la **aplicación** *(pl* aplicaciones)	program, app
la **banda ancha**	broadband
la **base de datos**	database
la **computadora (personal)** *(LAm)*	(personal) computer
la **computacíon en la nube**	cloud computing
la **copia de seguridad**	back-up
la **copia impresa**	print-out
la **dirección de correo (electrónico)** *(pl* direcciones ~ ~ (~))	email address
la **función** *(pl* funciones)	function
la **grabadora de DVD**	DVD writer
la **hoja de cálculo**	spreadsheet
la **interfaz** *(pl* interfaces)	interface
la **Internet**	Internet
la **llave USB**	USB key
la **memoria RAM**	RAM, random-access memory
la **memoria ROM**	ROM, read-only memory
la **nube**	cloud
la **página de inicio**	home page
la **pantalla**	screen
la **papelera de reciclaje**	recycle bin
la **red**	network
la **unidad de disco**	disk drive
la **ventana**	window
la **Web** *(pl* ~s)	Web
la **webcam** *(pl* ~s)	webcam

USEFUL PHRASES

copiar to copy; **eliminar, suprimir** to delete; **formatear** to format
descargar/subir un archivo to download/upload a file
guardar to save; **imprimir** to print; **teclear** to key
navegar por Internet to surf the internet; **inalámbrico** wireless

COUNTRIES

ESSENTIAL WORDS (*masculine*)

Canadá	Canada
EE.UU.	USA
Estados Unidos	United States
país	country
Países Bajos	Netherlands
Reino Unido	United Kingdom

USEFUL WORDS (*masculine*)

Brasil	Brazil
Ecuador	Ecuador
El Salvador	El Salvador
Japón	Japan
Marruecos	Morocco
México	Mexico
Pakistán	Pakistan
Panamá	Panama
Paraguay	Paraguay
Perú	Peru
Tercer Mundo	Third World
Túnez	Tunisia
Uruguay	Uruguay

USEFUL PHRASES

mi país de origen my native country
la capital de España the capital of Spain
¿de qué país eres (*or* es)? what country do you come from?
soy de (los) Estados Unidos/de Canadá I come from the United States/ from Canada
nací en Escocia I was born in Scotland
me voy a los Países Bajos I'm going to the Netherlands
acabo de regresar de (los) Estados Unidos I have just come back from the United States
los países en (vías de) desarrollo the developing countries
países de habla hispana Spanish-speaking countries

ESSENTIAL WORDS *(feminine)*

América	America
América del Sur	South America
Alemania	Germany
Bélgica	Belgium
Escocia	Scotland
España	Spain
Europa	Europe
Francia	France
Gran Bretaña	Great Britain
Holanda	Holland
Inglaterra	England
Irlanda (del Norte)	(Northern) Ireland
Italia	Italy
(el País de) Gales	Wales
Sudamérica	South America
Suiza	Switzerland
USA	USA

USEFUL WORDS *(feminine)*

África	Africa
Argelia	Algeria
Asia	Asia
Bolivia	Bolivia
Colombia	Colombia
Costa Rica	Costa Rica
Cuba	Cuba
Francia	France
Grecia	Greece
Guatemala	Guatemala
la **India**	India
Nicaragua	Nicaragua
la **República Dominicana**	the Dominican Republic
la **Unión Europea, UE**	the European Union, the EU
Venezuela	Venezuela

NATIONALITIES

ESSENTIAL WORDS *(masculine)*

un **alemán** (*pl* alemanes)	a German
un **americano**	an American
un **belga**	a Belgian
un **británico**	a Briton
un **canadiense**	a Canadian
un **escocés** (*pl* escoceses)	a Scot
un **español**	a Spaniard
un **europeo**	a European
un **francés** (*pl* franceses)	a Frenchman
un **galés** (*pl* galeses)	a Welshman
un **holandés** (*pl* holandeses)	a Dutchman
un **inglés** (*pl* ingleses)	an Englishman
un **irlandés** (*pl* irlandeses)	an Irishman
un **italiano**	an Italian
un **pakistaní** (*pl* ~es *or* ~s)	a Pakistani
un **suizo**	a Swiss (man *or* boy)

USEFUL PHRASES
(él) es irlandés he is Irish
(ella) es irlandesa she is Irish
la campiña irlandesa the Irish countryside
una ciudad irlandesa an Irish town

ESSENTIAL WORDS *(feminine)*

una	**alemana**	a German
una	**americana**	an American
una	**belga**	a Belgian
una	**británica**	a Briton, a British woman *or* girl
una	**canadiense**	a Canadian
una	**escocesa**	a Scot
una	**española**	a Spaniard
una	**europea**	a European
una	**francesa**	a Frenchwoman, a French girl
una	**galesa**	a Welshwoman, a Welsh girl
una	**holandesa**	a Dutchwoman, a Dutch girl
una	**inglesa**	an Englishwoman, an English girl
una	**irlandesa**	an Irishwoman, an Irish girl
una	**italiana**	an Italian
una	**pakistaní** *(pl ~es or ~s)*	a Pakistani
una	**suiza**	a Swiss girl *or* woman

USEFUL PHRASES

soy escocés – hablo inglés I am Scottish – I speak English
soy escocesa I am Scottish
un(a) extranjero(a) a foreigner
en el extranjero abroad
la nacionalidad nationality

USEFUL WORDS (*masculine*)

un	**africano**	an African
un	**antillano**	a West Indian
un	**árabe**	an Arab
un	**argelino**	an Algerian
un	**argentino**	an Argentinian
un	**boliviano**	a Bolivian
un	**brasileño**	a Brazilian
un	**chileno**	a Chilean
un	**chino**	a Chinese
un	**colombiano**	a Colombian
un	**costarricense**	a Costa Rican
un	**cubano**	a Cuban
un	**dominicano**	a Dominican
un	**ecuatoriano**	an Ecuadorean
un	**griego**	a Greek
un	**guatemalteco**	a Guatemalan
un	**indio**	an Indian
un	**japonés** (*pl* japoneses)	a Japanese
un	**marroquí** (*pl* ~es *or* ~s)	a Moroccan
un	**mexicano**	a Mexican
un	**nicaragüense**	a Nicaraguan
un	**panameño**	a Panamanian
un	**paraguayo**	a Paraguayan
un	**peruano**	a Peruvian
un	**ruso**	a Russian
un	**salvadoreño**	a Salvadorian
un	**tunecino**	a Tunisian
un	**turco**	a Turk
un	**uruguayo**	a Uruguayan
un	**venezolano**	a Venezuelan

USEFUL WORDS *(feminine)*

una **africana**	an African
una **antillana**	a West Indian
una **árabe**	an Arab
una **argelina**	an Algerian
una **argentina**	an Argentinian
una **boliviana**	a Bolivian
una **brasileña**	a Brazilian
una **chilena**	a Chilean
una **china**	a Chinese
una **colombiana**	a Colombian
una **costarricense**	a Costa Rican
una **cubana**	a Cuban
una **dominicana**	a Dominican
una **ecuatoriana**	an Ecuadorean
una **griega**	a Greek
una **guatemalteca**	a Guatemalan
una **india**	an Indian
una **japonesa**	a Japanese
una **marroquí** *(pl* ~es *or* ~s)	a Moroccan
una **mexicana**	a Mexican
una **nicaragüense**	a Nicaraguan
una **panameña**	a Panamanian
una **paraguaya**	a Paraguayan
una **peruana**	a Peruvian
una **rusa**	a Russian
una **salvadoreña**	a Salvadorian
una **tunecina**	a Tunisian
una **turca**	a Turk
una **uruguaya**	a Uruguayan
una **venezolana**	a Venezuelan

ESSENTIAL WORDS *(masculine)*

el	**aire**	air
el	**albergue juvenil**	youth hostel
el	**árbol**	tree
el	**arroyo**	stream
el	**bastón** *(pl bastones)*	walking stick
el	**bosque**	wood; forest
el	**camino**	way
el	**campesino**	countryman; farmer
el	**campo**	country; countryside
el	**castillo**	castle
el	**cazador**	hunter
el	**granjero**	farmer
el	**mercado**	market
el	**paisaje**	scenery
el	**paseo**	walk
el	**picnic** *(pl inv or ~s)*	picnic
el	**prado**	field
el	**pueblo**	village
el	**puente**	bridge
el	**río**	river
el	**ruido**	noise
el	**sendero**	path; track
el	**terreno**	soil; ground
el	**turista**	tourist
el	**valle**	valley

USEFUL PHRASES

al aire libre in the open air
sé el camino al pueblo I know the way to the village
salir en bicicleta to go cycling
los vecinos *or* **los habitantes de la zona** the locals
fuimos de picnic we went for a picnic

ESSENTIAL WORDS (*feminine*)

la **barrera**	gate; fence
la **camioneta** (*Sp*)	van
la **campesina**	countrywoman; farmer
la **carretera**	road
la **cazadora**	hunter
la **excursión** (*pl* excursiones)	hike
la **granja**	farm, farmhouse
la **granjera**	farmer
la **montaña**	mountain
la **piedra**	stone; rock
la **región** (*pl* regiones)	district
la **tierra**	land; earth; soil; ground
la **torre**	tower
la **turista**	tourist
la **vagoneta** (*Mex*)	van
la **valla**	fence

USEFUL PHRASES
en el campo in the country
ir (de excursión) al campo to go into the country
vivir en el campo/en la ciudad to live in the country/in town
cultivar la tierra to cultivate the land

IMPORTANT WORDS (*masculine*)

el	**agricultor** (*Sp*)	farmer
el	**guardia civil**	civil guard (*person*)
el	**lago**	lake
el	**mesón** (*pl* mesones)	inn
el	**polvo**	dust
el	**ranchero** (*Mex*)	farmer

USEFUL WORDS (*masculine*)

los	**anteojos de larga vista** (*LAm*)	binoculars
el	**arbusto**	bush
el	**barro**	mud
el	**brezo**	heather
el	**charco**	puddle
el	**estanque**	pond
el	**guijarro**	pebble
el	**heno**	hay
el	**matorral**	bush
el	**molino (de viento)**	(wind)mill
el	**palo**	stick
el	**pantano**	marsh
el	**páramo**	moor
el	**poste telegráfico**	telegraph pole
el	**prado**	meadow
los	**prismáticos** (*Sp*)	binoculars
el	**seto**	hedge
el	**trigo**	corn; wheat

USEFUL PHRASES

agrícola agricultural
apacible, tranquilo(a) peaceful
en la cima de la colina at the top of the hill
caer en una trampa to fall into a trap

IMPORTANT WORDS *(feminine)*

la	**agricultora** *(Sp)*	farmer
la	**agricultura**	agriculture
la	**calzada**	road surface
la	**catiusca, katiuska**	(wellington) boot
la	**cima**	top *(of hill)*
la	**colina**	hill
la	**gente del campo**	country people
la	**guardia civil**	civil guard *(person)*
la	**Guardia Civil**	Civil Guard
la	**hoja**	leaf
la	**posada**	inn
la	**propiedad**	property; estate
la	**ranchera** *(Mex)*	farmer
la	**tranquilidad**	peace

USEFUL WORDS *(feminine)*

la	**aldea**	hamlet
la	**bota de goma**	(wellington) boot
la	**cantera**	quarry
la	**cascada**	waterfall
la	**caverna**	cave
la	**caza**	hunting; shooting
la	**cosecha**	crop; harvest
la	**fuente**	spring; source
la	**furgoneta**	van
la	**llanura**	plain
la	**orilla**	bank *(of river)*
las	**ruinas**	ruins
la	**señal**	signpost
la	**trampa**	trap
la	**vendimia**	grape harvest
la	**zanja**	ditch

USEFUL PHRASES

perderse to lose one's way
recoger la cosecha to bring in the harvest
vendimiar, hacer la vendimia to harvest the grapes

ESSENTIAL WORDS (*masculine*)

el	**aspecto**	appearance
el	**bigote**	moustache
el	**cabello**	hair
el	**color**	colour
los	**ojos**	eyes
el	**talle**	waist

USEFUL PHRASES

alegre cheerful
alto(a) tall
amable nice
antiguo(a) old
asqueroso(a) disgusting
bajo(a) short
barbudo(a), con barba bearded, with a beard
bonito(a) pretty
bueno(a) kind
calvo(a) bald
delgado(a) skinny
desagradable unpleasant
dinámico(a) dynamic
divertido(a), entretenido(a) amusing, entertaining
educado(a) polite
esbelto(a) slim
estupendo(a) great
feliz (*pl* felices) happy
feo(a) ugly
gordo(a) fat
gracioso(a) funny
grosero(a) rude
guapo handsome; **guapa** beautiful
horrible hideous
infeliz (*pl* infelices), desgraciado(a) unhappy, unfortunate
inquieto(a) agitated
inteligente intelligent

ESSENTIAL WORDS *(feminine)*

la	**barba**	beard
la	**edad**	age
la	**estatura**	height; size
las	**gafas**	glasses
la	**identidad**	ID
la	**lágrima**	tear
la	**persona**	person
la	**talla**	size; height

USEFUL PHRASES

joven (*pl* **jóvenes**) young
largo(a) long
malo(a) naughty
mono(a) cute
nervioso(a), tenso(a) nervous, tense
optimista/pesimista optimistic/pessimistic
pequeño(a) small, little
que se porta bien well-behaved
serio(a) serious
tímido(a) shy
tonto(a) stupid
tranquilo(a) calm
viejo(a) old
(ella) parece triste she looks sad
(él) estaba llorando he was crying
(él) sonreía he was smiling
(él) tenía lágrimas en los ojos he had tears in his eyes
un hombre de estatura mediana a man of average height
mido 1 metro 70 *or* **uno setenta** *or* **1,70** I am 1 metre 70 tall
¿de qué color son tus (*or* sus) ojos/es tu (*or* su) pelo? what colour are your eyes/is your hair?
tengo el pelo rubio I have fair hair
tengo los ojos azules/verdes I have blue/green eyes
pelo moreno *or* **castaño** dark *or* brown hair
pelo castaño light brown hair; **pelo rizado** curly hair; **pelirrojo(a)** red-haired
pelo negro/canoso black/grey hair
pelo teñido dyed hair

IMPORTANT WORDS *(masculine)*

el	**carácter** *(pl* caracteres)	character; nature
el	**grano**	spot
el	**humor**	mood

USEFUL WORDS *(masculine)*

el	**cerquillo** *(LAm)*	fringe
el	**defecto**	fault
el	**fleco** *(Mex)*, el **flequillo** *(Sp)*	fringe
el	**gesto**	gesture
el	**gigante**	giant
los	**hoyuelos**	dimples
el	**lunar**	mole, beauty spot
el	**parecido**	resemblance
el	**peso**	weight
el	**rizo**	curl

USEFUL PHRASES

(él) tiene buen carácter he is good-tempered
(él) tiene mal genio *or* **carácter** he is bad-tempered
tener la tez pálida *or* **muy blanca** to have a pale complexion
llevar gafas/lentes de contacto *or* **lentillas** to wear glasses/contact lenses

IMPORTANT WORDS *(feminine)*

la	**belleza**	beauty
la	**calidad**	(good) quality
la	**costumbre**	habit
la	**curiosidad**	curiosity
la	**expresión** *(pl* expresiones)	expression
la	**fealdad**	ugliness
las	**lentillas**	contact lenses
la	**mirada**	look
la	**sonrisa**	smile
la	**tez** *(pl* teces)	complexion
la	**voz** *(pl* voces)	voice

USEFUL WORDS *(feminine)*

las	**arrugas**	wrinkles
la	**cicatriz** *(pl* cicatrices)	scar
la	**dentadura (postiza)**	false teeth
las	**pecas**	freckles
la	**permanente**	perm
la	**timidez**	shyness

USEFUL PHRASES

siempre estoy de buen humor I am always in a good mood
(él) está de mal humor he is in a bad mood
(él) se enfadó he got angry
(ella) se parece a su madre she looks like her mother
(él) se muerde las uñas he bites his nails

ESSENTIAL WORDS (*masculine*)

el	**alemán**	German
el	**alfabeto**	alphabet
el	**alumno**	pupil; schoolboy
el	**amigo**	pal
el	**aprendizaje**	apprenticeship
el	**club** (*pl* ~s *or* ~es)	club
el	**colegio**	school
el	**colegio de secundaria**	secondary school
el	**comedor**	dining hall
el	**comienzo del curso**	beginning of term
el	**compañero de clase**	school friend
el	**concierto**	concert
el	**cuaderno**	notebook; exercise book
los	**deberes**	homework
el	**día**	day
el	**dibujo**	drawing
el	**director**	headmaster
el	**dormitorio**	dormitory
el	**error**	mistake
el	**escolar**	schoolboy
el	**español**	Spanish
el	**estudiante**	student
el	**estudio (de)**	study (of)
los	**estudios**	studies
el	**examen** (*pl* exámenes)	exam
el	**examen de prueba** (*pl* exámenes ~~)	mock exam
el	**experimento**	experiment
el	**fallo**	mistake
el	**francés**	French
el	**gimnasio**	gym
el	**grupo**	group
el	**horario**	timetable
el	**IES (Instituto de Enseñanza Secundaria)**	comprehensive school
el	**inglés**	English
el	**instituto**	secondary school
el	**intercambio**	exchange
el	**italiano**	Italian

ESSENTIAL WORDS *(feminine)*

la **alberca** (*Mex*)	swimming pool
la **alumna**	pupil; schoolgirl
la **amiga**	pal
el **aula** (*pl f* las aulas)	classroom
la **biología**	biology
la **cafetería**	canteen
las **ciencias**	science
la **clase**	class; year; classroom
las **clases**	lessons
las **clases prácticas**	practical class
la **compañera de clase**	school friend
la **directora**	headmistress
la **educación física**	PE
la **electrónica**	electronics
la **enseñanza**	education; teaching
la **escolar**	schoolgirl
la **escuela**	school
la **escuela de primaria**	primary school
la **escuela infantil**	nursery school
la **estudiante**	student
la **excursión** (*pl* excursiones)	trip; outing
la **exposición** (*pl* exposiciones)	presentation
la **física**	physics
la **frase**	sentence
la **geografía**	geography
la **gimnasia**	gym
la **goma (de borrar)**	rubber
la **grabadora**	tape recorder
la **guardería**	nursery school
la **historia**	history; story
la **informática**	computer studies
la **lección** (*pl* lecciones)	lesson
la **lectura**	reading
las **lenguas (modernas)**	(modern) languages
la **maestra de primaria** *or* **de infantil**	primary schoolteacher
las **matemáticas**	mathematics
la **materia (escolar)**	(school) subject

ESSENTIAL WORDS *(masculine continued)*

el	**laboratorio**	laboratory
el	**lápiz** (*pl* lápices)	pencil
el	**libro**	book
el	**maestro de primaria** *or* **de infantil**	primary schoolteacher
el	**mapa**	map
el	**ordenador**	computer
el	**premio**	prize
el	**profesor**	teacher
el	**progreso**	progress
el	**recreo**	break; playtime
el	**resultado**	result
el	**semestre**	semester
el	**trabajo**	work
los	**trabajos manuales**	handicrafts

USEFUL PHRASES

trabajar to work

aprender to learn

estudiar to study

¿cuánto tiempo llevas (*or*** lleva) aprendiendo español?** how long have you been learning Spanish?

aprenderse algo de memoria to learn sth off by heart

tengo deberes/tareas todos los días *or* **a diario** I have homework every day

mi hermana pequeña va a primaria/al colegio – yo voy a secundaria *or* **al instituto** my little sister goes to primary school – I go to secondary school

enseñar español to teach Spanish

el/la profesor(a) de alemán the German teacher

he mejorado en matemáticas I have made progress in maths

hacer un examen to sit an exam

aprobar un examen to pass an exam

suspender un examen to fail an exam

sacar un aprobado to get a pass mark

ESSENTIAL WORDS *(feminine continued)*

las	**mates**	maths
la	**música**	music
la	**natación**	swimming
la	**nota**	mark
la	**palabra**	word
la	**piscina**	swimming pool
la	**pizarra**	blackboard
la	**pregunta**	question
la	**profesora**	teacher
la	**química**	chemistry
la	**respuesta**	answer
la	**sala de profesores**	staffroom
la	**tarea**	homework; task
la	**universidad**	university
las	**vacaciones**	holidays
las	**vacaciones de verano**	summer holidays

USEFUL PHRASES

fácil easy; **difícil** difficult
interesante interesting
aburrido(a) boring
leer to read; **escribir** to write
escuchar to listen (to)
mirar to look at, watch
repetir to repeat
responder to reply
hablar to speak
es la primera *or* **mejor de la clase** she is top of the class
es la última *or* **peor de la clase** she is bottom of the class
entrar en clase to go into the classroom
cometer un error *or* **fallo** to make a mistake
corregir to correct
cometí un error gramatical I made a grammatical error
he sacado buena nota I got a good mark
¡responde a la pregunta! answer the question!
¡levantad la mano! put your hand up!

IMPORTANT WORDS (masculine)

el **bachillerato**, el **bachiller**	higher school-leaving course/certificate
el **certificado**	certificate
el **colegio concertado**	grant-aided school
el **colegio privado**	private school
el **colegio público**	state school
el **despacho**	office
el **día libre**	day off
el **diploma**	diploma
el **estuche**	pencil case
el **examen escrito** (pl exámenes ~s)	written exam
el **examen oral** (pl exámenes ~es)	oral exam
el **expediente**	file
el **libro electrónico**	e-book
el **papel**	paper
el **pasillo**	corridor
el **patio (de recreo)**	playground

USEFUL PHRASES

mi amigo se está preparando la selectividad my friend is sitting his
   university entrance exam
repasar (la lección) to revise
repasaré otra vez la lección mañana I'll go over the lesson again
   tomorrow

IMPORTANT WORDS (*feminine*)

la	**ausencia**	absence
la	**carpeta**	folder; file
la	**conferencia**	lecture
las	**normas**	rules
las	**notas**	report
la	**oposición** (*pl* oposiciones)	competitive exam
la	**regla**	rule; ruler
la	**selectividad** (*Sp*)	entrance examination
la	**traducción** (*pl* traducciones)	translation
la	**versión** (*pl* versiones)	translation (*from foreign language to English*)

USEFUL PHRASES

en segundo de primaria in year two
en primero de ESO in year seven
en segundo de ESO in year eight
en tercero de ESO in year nine
en cuarto de ESO in year ten
en primero de bachillerato in year eleven

presente present
ausente absent
castigar a un(a) alumno(a) to punish a pupil
el/la profesor(a) los castigó sin recreo the teacher kept them in at break time
¡silencio!, ¡callaos! be quiet!

USEFUL WORDS *(masculine)*

el	**bedel**	janitor
el	**bloc** *(pl ~s)*	jotter
el	**boli, bolígrafo**	Biro®
el	**borrador**	rough copy
el	**cálculo**	sum
el	**castigo**	detention; punishment
el	**comportamiento**	behaviour
el	**corrector (líquido)**	correction fluid
el	**diccionario**	dictionary
el	**ejercicio**	exercise
el	**examinador**	examiner
el	**griego**	Greek
el	**jefe de estudios**	director of studies
el	**inspector**	school inspector
el	**internado**	boarding school
el	**interno**	boarder
el	**latín**	Latin
el	**libro de texto**	textbook
el	**maletín** *(pl maletines)*	briefcase
el	**parte (de faltas** *or* **ausencias)**	absence sheet
el	**parvulario**	nursery school
el	**profesor consejero**	form tutor
el	**pupitre**	desk
el	**rotulador**	felt-tip pen
el	**sacapuntas** *(pl inv)*	pencil sharpener
el	**test** *(pl ~s)*	test
el	**trabajo**	essay; class exam
el	**trimestre**	term
el	**vestuario**	cloakroom
el	**vocabulario**	vocabulary

USEFUL WORDS *(feminine)*

el	**álgebra** *(f)*	algebra
la	**aritmética**	arithmetic
la	**bedel**	janitor
la	**calculadora**	calculator
la	**caligrafía**	handwriting
la	**carpintería**	woodwork
la	**cartera**	satchel; schoolbag; briefcase
las	**ciencias del medio ambiente**	natural science
las	**ciencias naturales**	natural history
la	**enseñanza religiosa**	religious instruction
la	**entrega de premios**	prize-giving
la	**ESO (Educación Secundaria Obligatoria)** *(Sp)*	compulsory secondary education
la	**facultad**	faculty
la	**fila**	row *(of seats etc)*
la	**FP (formación profesional)** *(Sp)*	technical college
la	**geometría**	geometry
la	**gramática**	grammar
la	**inspectora**	school inspector
la	**interna**	boarder
la	**mancha**	blot
la	**nota media**	pass mark; average mark
la	**ortografía**	spelling
la	**pizarra (electrónica) interactiva**	interactive whiteboard
la	**poesía**	poetry; poem
la	**prueba**	test
las	**TIC (tecnologías de la información y la comunicación)**	ICT
la	**tinta**	ink
la	**tiza**	chalk
la	**traducción inversa** *(pl* traducciones ~s)	prose translation

ESSENTIAL WORDS *(masculine)*

el	**aerogenerador**	wind turbine
el	**agujero**	hole
el	**aire**	air
los	**animales**	animals
los	**árboles**	trees
el	**bosque**	wood
el	**coche**	car
el	**diesel**	diesel
el	**ecologista**	environmentalist
el	**gas**	gas
los	**gases de escape**	exhaust fumes
el	**gasoil**	diesel
los	**habitantes**	inhabitants
el	**mapa**	map
el	**mar**	sea
el	**medio ambiente**	environment
el	**mundo**	world
el	**país**	country
el	**pescado**	fish
el	**tiempo**	weather; time
los	**Verdes**	the Greens
el	**vidrio**	glass

IMPORTANT WORDS *(masculine)*

el	**biocombustible**	biofuel
el	**calor**	heat
el	**cambio climático**	climate change
el	**clima**	climate
el	**contaminante**	pollutant
el	**daño**	damage
el	**detergente**	detergent; washing powder
el	**gobierno**	government
el	**impuesto**	tax
el	**lago**	lake
el	**parque eólico**	windfarm
el	**planeta**	planet
el	**río**	river

ESSENTIAL WORDS *(feminine)*

el	**agua** *(f)*	water
las	**botellas**	bottles
la	**contaminación**	pollution
la	**costa**	coast
la	**cuestión** *(pl* cuestiones*)*	question
la	**ecología**	ecology
la	**especie**	species
la	**fábrica**	factory
la	**flor**	flower
la	**fruta**	fruit
la	**gasolina**	petrol
la	**isla**	island
la	**lluvia**	rain
la	**montaña**	mountain
la	**planta**	plant
la	**playa**	beach
la	**región** *(pl* regiones*)*	region; area
la	**temperatura**	temperature
la	**tierra**	earth
la(s)	**verdura(s)**	vegetables

IMPORTANT WORDS *(feminine)*

la	**central nuclear**	nuclear plant
la	**crisis** *(pl inv)*	crisis
la	**huella de carbono**	carbon footprint
la	**legumbre**	vegetable
la	**selva**	forest; jungle
la	**solución** *(pl* soluciones*)*	solution
la	**zona**	zone

USEFUL WORDS *(masculine)*

el	**acontecimiento**	event
el	**aerosol**	aerosol
los	**alimentos orgánicos**	organic food
el	**aluminio**	aluminium
el	**calentamiento global**	global warming
el	**canal**	canal
el	**catalizador**	catalytic converter
el	**CFC (clorofluorocarbono)**	CFC
los	**científicos**	scientists
el	**combustible**	fuel
el	**continente**	continent
el	**desarrollo sostenible**	sustainable development
el	**desierto**	desert
el	**ecosistema**	ecosystem
el	**fertilizante**	(artificial) fertilizer
el	**futuro**	future
el	**investigador**	researcher
el	**océano**	ocean
el	**OGM (organismo genéticamente modificado)**	GMO
el	**producto**	product
los	**productos químicos**	chemicals
el	**reciclado,** el **reciclaje**	recycling
los	**residuos nucleares/ industriales**	nuclear/industrial waste
el	**universo**	universe
el	**vertedero**	dumping ground

USEFUL PHRASES

(él) es muy respetuoso con el medio ambiente he's very environmentally-minded

un producto ecológico an eco-friendly product

en el futuro in the future

reciclar to recycle

salvar to save

verde green

hibrido hybrid

USEFUL WORDS *(feminine)*

las	**aguas residuales**	sewage
la	**capa de ozono**	ozone layer
la	**catástrofe**	disaster
la	**contaminación acústica**	noise pollution
la	**energía eólica**	wind power
la	**energía nuclear**	nuclear power
la	**energía renovable**	renewable energy
la	**lluvia ácida**	acid rain
la	**luna**	moon
la	**marea negra**	oil slick
la	**población** (*pl* poblaciones)	population
la	**selva tropical**	tropical rainforest

USEFUL PHRASES

biodegradable biodegradable

nocivo(a) *or* **dañino(a) para el medio ambiente** harmful to the environment

orgánico(a), biológico(a), ecológico(a) organic

gasolina sin plomo unleaded petrol

(las) especies en peligro de extinción endangered species

destruír to destroy

contaminar to contaminate; to pollute

prohibir to ban

ESSENTIAL WORDS (*masculine*)

el	**abuelo**	grandfather
los	**abuelos**	grandparents
los	**adultos**	adults
el	**apellido**	surname
el	**apellido de soltera**	maiden name
el	**bebé**	baby
la	**edad**	age
el	**hermano**	brother
el	**hijo**	son
el	**hombre**	man
el	**joven** (*pl* jóvenes)	youth, young man
los	**jóvenes**	young people
el	**marido**	husband
el	**niño**	child, boy
el	**nombre**	name
el	**nombre (de pila)**	first *or* Christian name
el	**novio**	fiancé
el	**padre**	father
los	**padres**	parents
el	**papá**	daddy
el	**pariente**	relative
el	**primo**	cousin
el	**prometido**	fiancé
el	**tío**	uncle

USEFUL PHRASES

¿qué edad tiene (*or* tienes)?, **¿cuántos años tiene (*or* tienes)?** how old are you?

tengo 15 años – él tiene 40 años I'm 15 – he is 40

¿cómo se llama (*or* te llamas)? what is your name?

me llamo Daniela my name is Daniela

él se llama Paco his name is Paco

prometido(a) engaged

casado(a) married

divorciado(a) divorced

separado(a) separated

casarse con algn to marry sb

casarse to get married; **divorciarse** to get divorced

ESSENTIAL WORDS (*feminine*)

la	**abuela**	grandmother
la	**familia**	family
la	**gente**	people
la	**hermana**	sister
la	**hija**	daughter; girl
la	**joven** (*pl* jóvenes)	youth
la	**madre**	mother
la	**mamá**	mummy
los	**mayores**	grown-ups
la	**mujer**	woman; wife
la	**niña**	child, girl
la	**novia**	fiancée
la	**persona**	person
la	**prima**	cousin
la	**prometida**	fiancée
la	**señora**	lady
la	**tía**	aunt

USEFUL PHRASES

más joven/mayor que yo younger/older than me

¿tiene (*or* tienes) hermanos? do you have any brothers or sisters?

tengo un hermano y una hermana I have one brother and one sister

no tengo hermanos I don't have any brothers or sisters

soy hijo(a) único(a) I am an only child

toda la familia the whole family

crecer to grow

envejecer, hacerse viejo(a) to get old

me llevo bien con mis padres I get on well with my parents

mi madre trabaja my mother works

IMPORTANT WORDS (*masculine*)

el	**adolescente**	teenager
el	**esposo**	husband
el	**nieto**	grandson
los	**nietos**	grandchildren
el	**padrastro**	stepfather
el	**sobrino**	nephew
el	**soltero**	bachelor
el	**subsidio familiar (por hijos)**	child benefit
el	**suegro**	father-in-law
el	**vecino**	neighbour
el	**viudo**	widower

USEFUL WORDS (*masculine*)

el	**ahijado**	godson
el	**anciano**	old man
el	**apodo**	nickname
el	**chaval**, el **chico**	kid
el	**cuñado**	brother-in-law
los	**gemelos**	identical twins
el	**hermanastro**	stepbrother
el	**hijastro**	stepson
el	**huérfano**	orphan
el	**jubilado**	pensioner
el	**marido**	bridegroom
los	**mellizos**	twins
el	**mote**	nickname
el	**padrino**	godfather
los	**recién casados**	newlyweds
los	**trillizos**	triplets
el	**viejo**	old man
el	**yerno**	son-in-law

USEFUL PHRASES

nacer to be born; **vivir** to live; **morir** to die
nací en 1990 I was born in 1990
mi abuela murió or **está muerta** my grandmother is dead
ella murió en 1995 she died in 1995

IMPORTANT WORDS (feminine)

la	**adolescente**	teenager
la	**au pair** (pl inv)	au pair girl
la	**esposa**	wife
la	**madrastra**	stepmother
la	**nieta**	granddaughter
la	**sobrina**	niece
la	**soltera**	single woman
la	**suegra**	mother-in-law
la	**vecina**	neighbour
la	**viuda**	widow

USEFUL WORDS (feminine)

la	**ahijada**	goddaughter
el	**ama de casa** (pl f las amas ~~)	housewife
la	**anciana**	old woman
la	**chavala**, la **chica**	kid
la	**cuñada**	sister-in-law
las	**gemelas**	identical twins
la	**hermanastra**	stepsister
la	**hijastra**	stepdaughter
la	**huérfana**	orphan
la	**jubilada**	pensioner
la	**madrina**	godmother
las	**mellizas**	twins, twin sisters
la	**niñera**	nanny
la	**novia**	bride
la	**nuera**	daughter-in-law
la	**pareja**	couple
la	**vejez**	old age
la	**vieja**	old woman

USEFUL PHRASES

él/ella es soltero(a) he/she is single
él es viudo he is a widower; **ella es viuda** she is a widow
soy el/la más joven I am the youngest; **soy el/la mayor** I am the eldest
mi hermana mayor my older sister

ESSENTIAL WORDS (*masculine*)

el	**agricultor** (*Sp*)	farmer
el	**animal**	animal
el	**bosque**	forest
el	**buey**	ox
el	**caballo**	horse
el	**cabrito**	kid
el	**campo**	field; country
el	**cerdo**	pig
el	**chivo**	kid
el	**gato**	cat
el	**granjero**	farmer
el	**invernadero**	greenhouse
el	**pato**	duck
el	**pavo**	turkey
el	**perro**	dog
el	**perro pastor** (*pl* ~s ~)	sheepdog
el	**pollo**	chicken
el	**pueblo**	village
el	**ranchero** (*Mex*)	farmer
el	**ternero**	calf

IMPORTANT WORDS (*masculine*)

el	**campesino**	countryman
el	**cordero**	lamb
el	**gallo**	cock
el	**tractor**	tractor

USEFUL PHRASES

un trigal, un maizal a cornfield
la agricultura ecológica organic farming
los pollos de granja free range chickens
los huevos de corral free range eggs
cuidar los animales to look after the animals
recolectar to harvest
recoger la cosecha to bring in the harvest/crops

ESSENTIAL WORDS *(feminine)*

la	**agricultora** *(Sp)*	farmer
la	**camioneta** *(Sp)*	van
la	**cerda**	sow
la	**finca**	farm
la	**gallina**	hen
la	**granja**	farm; farmhouse
la	**granjera**	farmer; farmer's wife
la	**oveja**	sheep; ewe
la	**puerta**	gate
la	**ranchera** *(Mex)*	farmer
la	**tierra**	earth; ground
la	**vaca**	cow
la	**vagoneta** *(Mex)*	van
la	**valla**	fence
la	**verja**	gate
la	**yegua**	mare

IMPORTANT WORDS *(feminine)*

la	**campesina**	countrywoman
la	**colina**	hill

USEFUL PHRASES
vivir en el campo to live in the country
trabajar en una granja to work on a farm
recolectar el heno to make hay

USEFUL WORDS (*masculine*)

el	**abono**	manure; fertilizer
el	**almiar**	haystack
el	**arado**	plough
el	**barro**	mud
el	**burro**	donkey
el	**carnero**	ram
el	**centeno**	rye
el	**cerdo**	pig
el	**cereal**	cereal, crop
el	**cobertizo**	shed
el	**corral**	farmyard
el	**espantapájaros** (*pl inv*)	scarecrow
el	**establo**	cow shed, byre
el	**estanque**	pond
el	**estiércol**	manure
el	**gallinero**	henhouse
el	**ganado**	cattle
el	**ganso**	goose
el	**granero**	barn
el	**grano**	grain, seed
el	**heno**	hay
el	**maíz** (*pl* maices)	maize
el	**molino (de viento)**	(wind)mill
el	**paisaje**	landscape
el	**pajar**	loft
el	**páramo**	moor, heath
el	**pastor**	shepherd
el	**pollito**	chick
el	**potro**	foal
el	**pozo**	well
el	**prado**	meadow
el	**rebaño**	(*sheep*) flock; (*cattle*) herd
el	**suelo**	ground, earth
el	**surco**	furrow
el	**toro**	bull
el	**trigo**	corn; wheat

USEFUL WORDS *(feminine)*

la	**avena**	oats
la	**cabra**	goat
la	**cabritilla**	kid
la	**carretilla**	cart
la	**casita (con el tejado de paja)**	(thatched) cottage
la	**cebada**	barley
la	**cosecha**	crop
la	**cosechadora**	combine harvester
la	**cuadra**	stable
la	**escalera**	ladder
la	**ganadería**	cattle farm
la	**lana**	wool
la	**lonja**	market
la	**paja**	straw
la	**pocilga**	pigsty
la	**recolección** (*pl* recolecciones)	harvest
la	**uva**	grapes
la	**vendimia**	grape harvest, grape picking
la	**viña**	vine
la	**zanja**	ditch

ESSENTIAL WORDS *(masculine)*

el **marisco**	seafood
el **pez** *(pl* peces*)*	fish
el **pez de colores** *(pl* peces ~ ~*)*	goldfish

IMPORTANT WORDS *(masculine)*

el **cangrejo**	crab
el **insecto**	insect

USEFUL WORDS *(masculine)*

el **acuario**	aquarium
el **arenque**	herring
el **atún** *(pl* atunes*)*	tuna
el **avispón** *(pl* avispones*)*	hornet
el **bacalao**	cod
el **calamar**	squid
el **camarón** *(pl* camarones*)*	shrimp
el **cangrejo de río**	crayfish
el **chinche**	bug
el **eglefino**	haddock
el **grillo**	cricket
el **gusano**	worm
el **gusano de seda**	silkworm
los **langostinos**	scampi
el **lenguado**	sole
el **lucio**	pike
el **mejillón** *(pl* mejillones*)*	mussel
el **mosquito**	mosquito
el **pulpo**	octopus
el **renacuajo**	tadpole
el **salmón** *(pl* salmones*)*	salmon
el **saltamontes** *(pl inv)*	grasshopper
el **tiburón** *(pl* tiburones*)*	shark

USEFUL PHRASES
nadar to swim
volar to fly
vamos a ir a pescar we're going fishing

ESSENTIAL WORDS (*feminine*)

el **agua** (*f*)	water

IMPORTANT WORDS (*feminine*)

la **mosca**	fly
la **sardina**	sardine
la **trucha**	trout

USEFUL WORDS (*feminine*)

la **abeja**	bee
el **ala** (*pl f* las alas)	wing
la **anguila**	eel
la **araña**	spider
la **avispa**	wasp
la **cigala**	crayfish
la **cigarra**	cicada
la **cucaracha**	cockroach
la **hormiga**	ant
la **langosta**	lobster
la **libélula**	dragonfly
la **mariposa**	butterfly
la **mariquita**	ladybird
la **medusa**	jellyfish
la **mosquilla**	midge
la **mosquita**	midge
la **oruga**	caterpillar
la **ostra**	oyster
la **pescadilla**	whiting
la **polilla**	moth
la **pulga**	flea
la **rana**	frog

USEFUL PHRASES
una picadura de avispa a wasp sting
una tela de araña a spider's web

ESSENTIAL WORDS (*masculine*)

el	**aceite**	oil
el	**agua mineral**	(mineral) water
el	**alcohol**	alcohol
el	**almuerzo**	lunch
el	**aperitivo**	aperitif
el	**arroz**	rice
el	**asado**	roast
el	**autoservicio**	self-service restaurant
el	**azúcar**	sugar
el	**bar**	bar
el	**bistec** (*pl inv or* ~s)	steak
el	**bol**	bowl
el	**bote**	tin, can
el	**café**	coffee; café
el	**café con leche**	coffee with milk
el	**café con más leche**	milky coffee
el	**camarero** (*Sp*)	waiter
los	**caramelos**	sweets
el	**cerdo**	pork
los	**cereales**	cereal
el	**chocolate (caliente)**	(hot) chocolate
el	**cocinero**	cook
el	**consomé**	soup
el	**croissant** *or* el **cruasán**	croissant
	(*pl* cruasanes)	
el	**cuarto**	quarter (*bottle/litre etc*)
el	**cuenco**	bowl
el	**cuchillo**	knife
el	**desayuno**	breakfast
el	**dueño**	owner
los	**entrantes**	hors d'œuvres, starters
el	**entrecot** (*pl inv or* ~s)	(entrecôte) steak
el	**filete**	steak
el	**helado**	ice cream
el	**huevo**	egg
el	**huevo duro** *or* **cocido**	hard-boiled egg
el	**huevo pasado por agua**	soft-boiled egg
el	**jamón** (*pl* jamones)	ham

ESSENTIAL WORDS *(feminine)*

la	**aceituna**	olive
la	**baguette** *(pl inv or ~s)*	French loaf
la	**bandeja**	tray
la	**bebida**	drink
la	**botella**	bottle
la	**caja**	box
la	**carne**	meat
la	**carne de vaca**	beef
la	**carta**	menu
la	**cena**	dinner
la	**cerveza**	beer
la	**Coca-Cola**® *(pl ~s)*	Coke®
la	**comida**	lunch; meal
la	**comida precocinada**	ready-made meal
	or **preparada**	
las	**conservas**	canned food
la	**cuchara**	spoon
la	**cuenta**	bill
la	**ensalada**	salad
la	**ensalada mixta**	mixed salad
la	**fruta**	fruit
el	**hambre** *(f)*	hunger
la	**hamburguesa**	hamburger
la	**lata**	tin, can
la	**leche**	milk
la	**limonada**	lemonade
la	**loncha (de)**	slice (of)
la	**mantequilla**	butter
la	**mermelada**	jam
la	**mermelada (de cítricos)**	marmalade
la	**mesa**	table
la	**pastelería**	pastry; cake shop
las	**patatas fritas**	chips; crisps
la	**pescadería**	fish shop
la	**pieza de fruta**	piece of fruit
la	**repostería**	pastry; cake shop
la	**sal**	salt
la	**salchicha**	sausage

ESSENTIAL WORDS *(masculine continued)*

el	**marisco**	seafood
el	**menú del día**	fixed-price menu
el	**mesero** *(LAm)*	waiter
el	**pan**	bread
el	**paté**	pâté
el	**pescado**	fish
el	**picnic** *(pl inv or ~s)*	picnic
el	**platillo**	saucer
el	**plato**	plate; dish; course
el	**plato del día**	today's special
el	**pollo (asado)**	(roast) chicken
el	**postre**	dessert
el	**primero**, el **primer plato**	first course, starter
el	**queso**	cheese
el	**quiche** *(pl inv)*	quiche
el	**restaurante**	restaurant
el	**salami**, el **salchichón** *(pl salchichones)*	salami
el	**sándwich** *(pl ~s or ~es)*	sandwich
el	**self-service** *(pl inv)*	self-service restaurant
el	**servicio**	service
el	**té**	tea
el	**tenedor**	fork
el	**vaso**	glass
el	**vinagre**	vinegar
el	**vino**	wine
el	**yogur(t)**	yoghurt
el	**zumo de fruta**	fruit juice

USEFUL PHRASES

cocinar to cook; **comer** to eat
beber to drink; **tragar** to swallow
mi plato favorito my favourite dish
¿qué vas (*or* **va) a beber?** what are you having to drink?
está bueno *or* **rico** it's nice
estar hambriento, tener hambre to be hungry
estar sediendo, tener sed to be thirsty

ESSENTIAL WORDS *(feminine continued)*

la	**sed** *(pl inv)*	thirst
la	**sidra**	cider
la	**sopa**	soup
la	**tarta**	cake
la	**taza**	cup
la	**ternera**	veal
la	**tortilla francesa**	omelette
la	**tortita**	pancake
la	**tostada**	toast
la	**vajilla**	dishes
las	**verduras**	vegetables

IMPORTANT WORDS *(feminine)*

la	**cafetería**	cafeteria
la	**camarera**	waitress
la	**carne asada** *or* **a la parrilla**	grilled meat
la	**cerveza de barril**	draught beer
la	**chef** *(pl inv or ~s)*	chef
la	**chuleta de cerdo**	pork chop
la	**cucharilla**	teaspoon
la	**cucharita (de postre)**	dessertspoon
la	**cuchara de servir**	tablespoon
la	**garrafa**	carafe
la	**harina**	flour
la	**jarra**	jug
la	**mayonesa**	mayonnaise
la	**mostaza**	mustard
la	**nata**	cream
las	**patatas fritas (de bolsa)**	crisps
la	**pimienta**	pepper
la	**pizza**	pizza
la	**propina**	tip
la	**receta**	recipe
la	**selección** *(pl selecciones)*	choice
la	**tarta**	tart
la	**tetera**	teapot
la	**vainilla**	vanilla

IMPORTANT WORDS (*masculine*)

el	**ajo**	garlic
el	**almíbar**	syrup
el	**aperitivo**	snack
el	**camarero**	waiter
los	**caracoles**	snails
el	**carrito**	trolley
el	**chef** (*pl inv or* ~s)	chef
el	**cocinero jefe**	chef
el	**comercio justo**	fair trade
el	**conejo**	rabbit
el	**cordero**	lamb; mutton
el	**cubierto**	cover charge; place setting
el	**gusto**	taste
el	**olor**	smell
el	**precio con todo incluido**	inclusive price
el	**precio fijo**	set price
el	**refresco concentrado**	cordial
el	**restaurante**	restaurant
el	**sabor**	flavour
el	**suplemento**	extra charge
el	**tentempié**	snack

USEFUL WORDS (*masculine*)

el	**abrelatas** (*pl inv*)	tin opener
el	**aperitivo**	snack
el	**beicon**	bacon
el	**biscote**	Melba toast
el	**bollito**	roll
el	**bollo**	bun
el	**cacao**	cocoa
el	**champán** (*pl* champanes)	champagne
el	**coñac** (*pl inv*)	brandy
el	**corcho**	cork
el	**cubito (de hielo)**	ice cube
el	**estofado**	stew
el	**foie gras** (*pl inv*)	liver pâté
el	**hígado**	liver
el	**ketchup** (*pl inv*)	ketchup

USEFUL WORDS *(feminine)*

las	**aves**	poultry
la	**carta de vinos**	wine list
la	**caza**	game
la	**chuleta**	chop
la	**clara**	shandy
la	**comida**	food
la	**gelatina**	jelly
la	**infusión** (*pl* infusiones)	herbal tea
la	**jarra**	jug
la	**margarina**	margarine
la	**miel**	honey
la	**miga**	crumb
la	**nata montada**	whipped cream
las	**natillas**	custard
la	**pajita**	straw
la	**pasta**	pasta
la	**rebanada**	piece of bread and butter
la	**salsa**	sauce
la	**salsa de jugo de carne**	gravy
la	**servilleta**	napkin
la	**tisana**	herbal tea
las	**tripas**	tripe
la	**tostada**	slice of toast
la	**vinagreta**	vinaigrette dressing

USEFUL PHRASES

fregar los platos to do the dishes

cuando volvemos del colegio merendamos we have a snack when we come back from school

desayunar, tomar el desayuno to have breakfast

delicioso(a) delicious; **repugnante** disgusting

¡que aproveche! enjoy your meal!; **¡salud!** cheers!

¡la cuenta, por favor! the bill please!

"servicio (no) incluido" "service (not) included"

comer fuera to eat out

invitar a algn a comer to invite sb to lunch

tomar algo de beber, beber algo to have drinks

USEFUL WORDS *(masculine continued)*

el	**mantel**	tablecloth
los	**mejillones**	mussels
el	**panecillo**	roll
el	**paté de carne**	potted meat
el	**paté de hígado**	liver pâté
el	**paté de oca**	goose pâté
el	**puré de patatas**	mashed potatoes
los	**riñones**	kidneys
el	**rosbif** *(pl inv or ~s)*	roast beef
el	**sacacorchos** *(pl inv)*	corkscrew
el	**tapón** *(pl tapones)*	cork
el	**termo**	flask
el	**torrezno**	diced bacon
el	**whisky, whiskey** *(pl ~s)*	whisky
el	**zumo natural de limón**	freshly-squeezed lemon juice

USEFUL PHRASES

poner la mesa to set the table; **quitar la mesa** to clear the table
comer, almorzar to have lunch
cenar to have dinner
probar algo to taste sth
¡eso huele bien! that smells good!
vino blanco/rosado/tinto white/rosé/red wine
un filete poco hecho/en su punto/bien hecho a rare/medium/
    well-done steak
un sándwich (tostado) de jamón y queso a ham and cheese toastie

SMOKING

el	**cenicero**	ashtray
la	**cerilla**	match
el	**cigarrillo**	cigarette
el	**cigarro**	cigar
el	**estanco**	tobacconist's
el	**mechero**	lighter
la	**pipa**	pipe
el	**tabaco**	tobacco

USEFUL PHRASES

una caja de cerillas a box of matches
¿tienes (or tiene) fuego? do you have a light?
encender un cigarrillo to light up
"prohibido fumar" "no smoking"
no fumo I don't smoke
he dejado de fumar, he dejado el tabaco I've stopped smoking
fumar es perjudicial para tí or la salud smoking is very bad for you

ESSENTIAL WORDS *(masculine)*

el	**ajedrez**	chess
el	**amigo por correspondencia**	pen friend
el	**baile**	dance
el	**billete** *(Sp)*	ticket
el	**boleto** *(LAm)*	ticket
el	**cantante**	singer
el	**canto**	singing
el	**CD** *(pl inv or ~s)*	CD
el	**cine**	cinema
el	**club** *(pl ~s or ~es)*	club
el	**concierto**	concert
los	**deportes**	sports
el	**dinero de bolsillo**	pocket money
el	**disco**	record
el	**DVD** *(pl inv or ~s)*	DVD
el	**espectáculo**	show
el	**fin de semana**	weekend
el	**folleto**	leaflet
el	**futbolín** *(pl futbolines)*	table football
el	**hobby** *(pl hobbies)*	hobby
el	**Internet**	internet
el	**juego**	game
el	**lector de CD/DVD/MP3**	CD/DVD/MP3 player
el	**miembro**	member
el	**museo**	museum; art gallery
el	**paseo**	walk
el	**periódico**	newspaper
el	**programa**	programme
el	**teatro**	theatre
el	**(teléfono) móvil** *(Sp)* or **celular** *(LAm)*	mobile (phone)
el	**tiempo libre**	free time
el	**videojuego**	video game
el	**walkman®** *(pl ~s)*	personal stereo

ESSENTIAL WORDS (feminine)

la	**afición** (pl aficiones)	hobby
la	**amiga por correspondencia**	pen friend
la	**cadena de televisión**	TV channel
la	**cámara (de fotos)**	camera
la	**canción** (pl canciones)	song
la	**cantante**	singer
las	**cartas**	cards
la	**disco(teca)**	disco
la	**diversión** (pl diversiones)	entertainment
la	**estrella (de cine)** (m+f)	(film) star
la	**excursión** (pl excursiones)	trip; outing; hike
la	**fiesta**	party
la	**foto**	photo
la	**historieta**	comic strip
la	**lectura**	reading
la	**música (pop/clásica)**	(pop/classical) music
las	**noticias**	news
la	**novela**	novel
la	**novela policíaca** or **policiaca**	detective novel
la	**película**	film
la	**pista de patinaje**	skating rink
la	**prensa**	the press
la	**publicidad**	publicity
la	**radio**	radio
la	**revista**	magazine
la	**tele(visión)** (pl teles, televisiones)	television, TV
la	**videoconsola**	games console

USEFUL PHRASES

salgo con mis amigos I go out with my friends
leo el periódico I read the newspaper
veo la televisión I watch television
juego al fútbol/al tenis/a las cartas I play football/tennis/cards
hacer bricolaje to do DIY
hacer de canguro to baby-sit
hacer zapping to channel-hop
ir de discoteca or **marcha** (Sp) to go clubbing

IMPORTANT WORDS *(masculine)*

el	**anuncio**	notice; poster
los	**anuncios por palabras**	adverts; small ads
el	**carrete**	film *(for camera)*
el	**compact disc** *(pl ~~s)*	compact disc, CD
el	**concurso**	competition
los	**dibujos animados**	cartoon
el	**juguete**	toy
el	**mensaje de texto**	text message
el	**noticiero** *(LAm)*	news
el	**novio**	boyfriend
el	**ordenador (personal)** *(Sp)*	personal computer
los	**pasatiempos**	leisure activities
el	**PC** *(pl inv)*	PC
el	**programa**	programme
el	**punto**	knitting
el	**SMS** *(pl inv)*	text message
el	**telediario** *(Sp)*	news
el	**vídeo** *(Sp)*, el **video** *(LAm)*	video recorder
el	**website**	website

USEFUL WORDS *(masculine)*

el	**aficionado**	fan
el	**blog**	blog
el	**campamento de verano**	holiday camp
el	**chat**	chat; chatroom
el	**club nocturno** *(pl ~s or ~es ~s)*	night club
el	**coro**	choir
el	**crucigrama**	crossword puzzle(s)
el	**explorador**	scout
el	**juego de mesa**	board game
el	**monopatín** *(pl monopatines)*	skateboard
el	**videoclub** *(pl ~s or ~es)*	video shop

USEFUL PHRASES
emocionante exciting
aburrido(a) boring
divertido(a) funny

IMPORTANT WORDS *(feminine)*

la	**cámara digital**	digital camera
la	**casa de la juventud**	youth club
la	**cinta**	tape
la	**cinta de vídeo**	video cassette
la	**colección** *(pl* colecciones)	collection
la	**computadora (personal)** *(LAm)*	personal computer
la	**exposición** *(pl* exposiciones)	exhibition
la	**filmadora** *(LAm)*	camcorder
la	**grabadora de CD/DVD**	CD/DVD writer
la	**noche**	evening
la	**novia**	girlfriend
la	**pintura**	painting
la	**reunión** *(pl* reuniones)	meeting
la	**serie**	serial
la	**tarde**	evening
la	**telenovela**	soap (opera)
la	**videocámara** *(Sp)*	camcorder

USEFUL WORDS *(feminine)*

la	**aficionada**	fan
la	**diapositiva**	slide
la	**exploradora**	(girl) guide, girl scout
la	**fotografía**	photograph; photography
la	**lista de éxitos**	charts

USEFUL PHRASES

no está mal it's not bad
bastante bien quite good
bailar to dance
hacer fotos to take photos
estoy aburrido(a) I'm bored
quedamos los viernes we meet on Fridays
estoy ahorrando para comprarme un DVD I'm saving up to buy a DVD
me gustaría dar la vuelta al mundo I'd like to go round the world

ESSENTIAL WORDS *(masculine)*

el **albaricoque**	apricot
el **limón** *(pl* limones)	lemon
el **melocotón** *(pl* melocotones)	peach
el **plátano**	banana
el **pomelo**	grapefruit
el **tomate**	tomato

IMPORTANT WORDS *(masculine)*

el **árbol frutal**	fruit tree
el **melón** *(pl* melones)	melon

USEFUL WORDS *(masculine)*

el **aguacate**	avocado
el **anacardo**	cashew nut
el **arándano**	blueberry
el **cacahuete**	peanut
el **coco**	coconut
el **dátil**	date
el **higo**	fig
el **hueso**	stone *(in fruit)*
el **kiwi**	kiwi fruit
el **ruibarbo**	rhubarb

ESSENTIAL WORDS *(feminine)*

la	**castaña (asada)**	(roasted) chestnut
la	**cereza**	cherry
la	**frambuesa**	raspberry
la	**fresa**	strawberry
la	**fruta**	fruit
la	**manzana**	apple
la	**naranja**	orange
la	**pasa**	raisin
la	**pera**	pear
la	**piel**	skin
la	**(pieza de) fruta**	(piece of) fruit
la	**piña**	pineapple
la	**uva**	grape(s)

USEFUL WORDS *(feminine)*

la	**avellana**	hazelnut
la	**baya**	berry
la	**ciruela**	plum
la	**ciruela pasa**	prune
la	**granada**	pomegranate
la	**grosella espinosa**	gooseberry
la	**grosella negra**	blackcurrant
la	**grosella (roja)**	redcurrant
la	**mandarina**	tangerine
la	**mora**	blackberry
la	**nuez** *(pl* nueces)	nut; walnut
la	**pepita**	pip *(in fruit)*
la	**vid**	vine

USEFUL PHRASES

un zumo de naranja/piña an orange/a pineapple juice
un racimo de uvas a bunch of grapes
maduro(a) ripe
verde unripe
pelar una fruta to peel a fruit
resbalar al pisar una cáscara de plátano to slip on a banana skin

ESSENTIAL WORDS (masculine)

el	**armario** (Sp)	cupboard; wardrobe
el	**calefactor**	heater
el	**congelador**	freezer
el	**equipo (de música)**	stereo system
el	**espejo**	mirror
el	**frigo**	fridge
el	**frigorífico** (Sp)	fridge
el	**mueble**	piece of furniture
los	**muebles**	furniture
el	**radiodespertador**	radio alarm
el	**refrigerador** (LAm)	fridge
el	**reloj**	clock
el	**ropero** (LAm)	cupboard; wardrobe
el	**sillón** (pl sillones)	armchair
el	**teléfono**	telephone
el	**transistor**	transistor

IMPORTANT WORDS (masculine)

el	**aparador**	sideboard
el	**aparato**	appliance
el	**casete**	tape recorder
el	**cuadro**	picture
el	**escritorio**	(writing) desk
el	**hervidor**	kettle
el	**horno microondas**	microwave oven
el	**inalámbrico**	cordless phone
el	**lavavajillas** (pl inv)	dishwasher
el	**lector de CD/DVD**	CD/DVD player
el	**lector de libros electrónicos**	ereader
el	**libro electrónico**	e-book
el	**piano**	piano
el	**portátil**	laptop
el	**reproductor MP3**	MP3 player
el	**sofá**	sofa
el	**(teléfono) móvil** (Sp) or **celular** (LAm)	mobile phone
el	**vídeo** (Sp), el **video** (LAm)	video recorder

ESSENTIAL WORDS (*feminine*)

la	**balda**	shelf
la	**cama**	bed
la	**cocina (eléctrica/de gas)**	(electric/gas) cooker
la	**estufa**	heater
la	**habitación** (*pl* habitaciones)	room
la	**lámpara**	lamp
la	**lavadora**	washing machine
la	**mesa**	table
la	**pantalla (de lámpara)**	lampshade
la	**radio**	radio
la	**silla**	chair
la	**televisión** (*pl* televisiones)	television

IMPORTANT WORDS (*feminine*)

el	**arca** (*f pl* las arcas)	chest
la	**aspiradora**	vacuum cleaner
la	**librería**	bookcase
la	**mesa de centro**	coffee table
la	**pintura**	painting
la	**plancha**	iron
la	**radio digital**	digital radio
la	**secadora**	tumble-dryer
la	**tableta**	tablet

USEFUL WORDS (*masculine*)

la	**altavoz** (*pl* altavoces)	loudspeaker
el	**asiento**	seat
el	**cajón** (*pl* cajones)	drawer
el	**camión de mudanzas**	removal van
	(*pl* camiones ~ ~)	
el	**cargador**	charger
el	**carrito**	trolley
el	**colchón** (*pl* colchones)	mattress
el	**contestador**	answering machine
el	**horno**	oven
el	**mando a distancia**	remote control
el	**marco**	frame
el	**mobiliario**	furniture
el	**navegador (GPS)**	sat nav
el	**operario de mudanzas**	removal man
el	**paragüero**	umbrella stand
el	**peso**	scales
los	**postigos**	shutters
el	**robot de cocina** (*pl* ~ s ~ ~)	food processor
el	**secador (de pelo)**	hairdryer
el	**taburete**	stool
el	**teléfono inalámbrico**	cordless telephone
el	**tocador**	dressing table

USEFUL PHRASES
un apartamento *or* **piso amueblado** a furnished flat
encender/apagar el calefactor *or* **la estufa** to switch the heater on/off
he hecho la cama I've made my bed
sentarse to sit down
poner *or* **meter algo en el horno** to put sth in the oven
correr las cortinas to draw the curtains
cerrar los postigos *or* **las contraventanas** to close the shutters

USEFUL WORDS *(feminine)*

la	**alfombra**	rug
la	**antena**	aerial
la	**antena parabólica**	satellite dish
la	**cadena de música**	music centre
la	**cámara cinematográfica**	cine camera
la	**cómoda**	chest of drawers
las	**contraventanas**	shutters
la	**cuna**	cradle; cot
la	**estantería**	shelves
la	**lámpara de pie**	standard lamp
la	**lámpara halógena**	halogen lamp
las	**literas**	bunk beds
la	**máquina de coser**	sewing machine
la	**máquina de escribir**	typewriter
la	**memoria USB**	USB stick
la	**mesilla de noche**	bedside table
la	**moqueta**	fitted carpet
la	**mudanza**	move
la	**persiana**	blind
la	**plancha de pelo**	hair straighteners
la	**tabla de planchar**	ironing board
la	**videocámara**	video camera, camcorder

USEFUL PHRASES

es un piso de 4 habitaciones it's a 4-roomed flat

¡ya está el desayuno/la comida/la cena! breakfast/lunch/dinner is ready!

ESSENTIAL WORDS

los	**Alpes**	the Alps
	Andalucía	Andalusia
el	**Atlántico**	the Atlantic
	Barcelona	Barcelona
	Bruselas	Brussels
	Castilla	Castile
	Cataluña	Catalonia
la	**Costa del Sol**	the Costa del Sol
el	**este**	the east
las	**Islas Baleares**	the Balearic Islands
las	**Islas Canarias**	the Canary Islands
la	**Coruña**	Corunna
	Londres	London
	Málaga	Malaga
	Mallorca	Majorca
el	**Mar Cantábrico**	the Bay of Biscay
el	**Mediterráneo**	the Mediterranean
	Menorca	Minorca
el	**norte**	the north
el	**oeste**	the west
el	**País Vasco**	the Basque Country
el	**Peñón (de Gibraltar)**	the Rock (of Gibraltar)
los	**Pirineos**	the Pyrenees
	Sevilla	Seville
la	**sierra**	mountain range
el	**sur**	the south
	Vizcaya	Biscay
	Zaragoza	Saragossa

IMPORTANT WORDS

	Edimburgo	Edinburgh
el	**Támesis**	the Thames

USEFUL WORDS

	Atenas	Athens
	Berlín	Berlin
la	**capital**	capital
la	**comunidad autónoma**	autonomous region (*of Spain*)
el	**Extremo Oriente**	the Far East
	Ginebra	Geneva
las	**Islas Británicas**	the British Isles
la	**Haya**	The Hague
	Lisboa	Lisbon
	Marruecos	Morocco
	Moscú	Moscow
el	**Oriente Medio**	the Middle East
el	**Oriente Próximo**	the Near East
el	**Pacífico**	the Pacific
	París	Paris
	Pekín	Beijing
el	**Polo Norte/Sur**	the North/South Pole
la	**provincia**	province
	Roma	Rome
	Varsovia	Warsaw
	Venecia	Venice
	Viena	Vienna

USEFUL PHRASES

ir a Londres/Sevilla to go to London/Seville
ir a Andalucía to go to Andalusia
vengo de Barcelona/del País Vasco I come from Barcelona/the Basque Country

en el *or* **al norte** in *or* to the north
en el *or* **al sur** in *or* to the south
en el *or* **al este** in *or* to the east
en el *or* **al oeste** in *or* to the west

GREETINGS

hola hello
¿cómo está usted (*or* estás)? how are you?
¿qué tal? how are you?
bien fine (*in reply*)
encantado(a) pleased to meet you
¿dígame? hello (*on telephone*)
buenas tardes good afternoon; good evening
buenas noches good evening; good night
adiós goodbye; hello (*when passing one another*)
hasta mañana see you tomorrow
hasta luego see you later

BEST WISHES

feliz cumpleaños happy birthday
feliz Navidad merry Christmas
feliz Año Nuevo happy New Year
felices Pascuas happy Easter
recuerdos best wishes
saludos best wishes
bienvenido(a) welcome
enhorabuena congratulations
que aproveche enjoy your meal
que le vaya (*or* te vaya) bien all the best
que te diviertas (*or* se divierta) enjoy yourself
buena suerte good luck
buen viaje safe journey
jesús bless you (*after a sneeze*)
salud cheers
a tu (*or* vuestra, *etc*) salud good health

SURPRISE

Dios mío my goodness
¿qué?, ¿cómo? what?
entiendo oh, I see
vaya well, well
pues… well…
(¿)de verdad(?), (¿)sí(?) really(?)
(¿)estás (or está) de broma(?) you're kidding; are you kidding?
¡qué suerte! how lucky!

POLITENESS

perdone I'm sorry; excuse me
por favor please
gracias thank you
no, gracias no thank you
sí, gracias yes please
de nada not at all, don't mention it, you're welcome
con mucho gusto gladly

AGREEMENT

sí yes
por supuesto of course
de acuerdo, vale (*Sp*) OK
bueno fine

DISAGREEMENT

no no
que no no (*contradicting a positive statement*)
que sí yes (*contradicting a negative statement*)
claro que no of course not
ni hablar no way
en absoluto not at all
al contrario on the contrary
no me digas well I never
qué cara what a cheek
no te metas en lo que no te importa mind your own business

DIFFICULTIES

socorro help
fuego fire
ay ouch
perdón (I'm) sorry, excuse me, I beg your pardon
lo siento I'm sorry
qué pena what a pity
qué pesadez, qué rollo what a nuisance; how boring
estoy harto(a) I'm fed up
no aguanto más I can't stand it any more
vaya (por Dios) oh dear
qué horror how awful

ORDERS

cuidado be careful
para (or pare) stop
oiga, usted hey, you there
fuera de aquí clear off
silencio shh
basta ya that's enough
prohibido fumar no smoking
vamos, venga come on, let's go
sigue go ahead, go on
vámonos let's go

OTHERS

no tengo (ni) idea no idea
quizá, quizás perhaps, maybe
no (lo) sé I don't know
¿qué desea? can I help you?
aquí tienes there, there you are
ya voy just coming
no te preocupes don't worry
no merece la pena it's not worth it
a propósito by the way
cariño, querido(a) darling
el (or la) pobre poor thing
tanto mejor so much the better
no me importa I don't mind
a mí me da igual it's all the same to me
mala suerte too bad
depende it depends
¿qué voy a hacer? what shall I do?
¿para qué? what's the point?
me molesta it annoys me
me saca de quicio it gets on my nerves

ESSENTIAL WORDS *(masculine)*

el	**accidente**	accident
el	**dentista**	dentist
el	**doctor**	doctor
el	**enfermero**	(male) nurse
el	**enfermo**	patient
el	**estómago**	stomach
el	**hospital**	hospital
el	**médico**	doctor

IMPORTANT WORDS *(masculine)*

el	**algodón (hidrófilo)**	cotton wool
el	**antiséptico**	antiseptic
el	**comprimido**	tablet
el	**dolor**	pain
el	**esparadrapo**	(sticking) plaster
el	**farmacéutico**	chemist
el	**jarabe**	syrup
el	**medicamento**	medicine, drug
el	**paciente**	patient
el	**resfriado**	cold
el	**seguro**	insurance

USEFUL PHRASES

ha habido un accidente there's been an accident
ingresar en el hospital to be admitted to hospital
debe permanecer en cama you must stay in bed
estar enfermo(a) to be ill; **sentirse mejor** to feel better
cuidar to look after
me he hecho daño I have hurt myself
me he hecho un corte en el dedo I have cut my finger
me he torcido el tobillo I have sprained my ankle
se ha roto el brazo he has broken his arm
me he quemado I have burnt myself
me duele la garganta/la cabeza/ el estómago I've got a sore throat/
  a headache/a stomach ache
tener fiebre to have a temperature

ESSENTIAL WORDS *(feminine)*

la	**aspirina**	aspirin
la	**cama**	bed
la	**cita**	appointment
la	**dentista**	dentist
la	**doctora**	doctor
la	**enferma**	patient
la	**enfermera**	nurse
la	**farmacia**	chemist's *(shop)*
la	**médico**	doctor
la	**pastilla**	tablet, pill
la	**salud**	health
la	**temperatura**	temperature

IMPORTANT WORDS *(feminine)*

la	**ambulancia**	ambulance
la	**camilla**	stretcher
la	**clínica**	clinic, private hospital
la	**consulta**	surgery
la	**crema**	cream, ointment
la	**cucharada**	spoonful
la	**diarrea**	diarrhoea
la	**enfermedad**	illness
la	**escayola**	plaster cast
la	**farmacéutica**	chemist
la	**gripe**	flu
la	**gripe A**	swine flu
la	**herida**	wound, injury
la	**inyección** *(pl inyecciones)*	injection
la	**medicina**	medicine
la	**operación** *(pl operaciones)*	operation
la	**paciente**	patient
la	**píldora**	pill; the Pill
las	**quemaduras del sol**	sunburn
la	**receta**	prescription
la	**sangre**	blood
la	**tableta**	tablet
las	**urgencias**	Accident and Emergency
la	**venda**	bandage

USEFUL WORDS *(masculine)*

el	**absceso**	abscess
el	**acné**	acne
el	**arañazo**	scratch
el	**ataque**	fit
el	**ataque al corazón**	heart attack
el	**cáncer**	cancer
el	**cardenal**	bruise
el	**embarazo**	pregnancy
el	**estrés**	stress
el	**mareo**	dizzy spell; sickness
el	**microbio**	germ
el	**nervio**	nerve
el	**preservativo**	condom
los	**primeros auxilios**	first aid
el	**pulso**	pulse
el	**régimen**	diet
el	**reposo**	rest
el	**SAMU**	emergency medical service
el	**sarampión**	measles
el	**shock**	shock
el	**sida**	AIDS
el	**tónico**	tonic
el	**vendaje**	dressing
el	**veneno**	poison

USEFUL PHRASES

tengo sueño I'm sleepy
tengo naúseas I feel sick
adelgazar to lose weight
curar to cure
curarse to get better
engordar to put on weight
tragar to swallow
sangrar to bleed
toser to cough
vomitar to vomit
estar en forma to be in good shape
reposar, descansar to rest

USEFUL WORDS (*feminine*)

la	**amigdalitis**	tonsillitis
las	**anginas**	sore throat; tonsillitis
la	**apendicitis**	appendicitis
la	**astilla**	splinter
la	**cicatriz** (*pl* cicatrices)	scar
la	**dentadura postiza**	false teeth
la	**dieta**	diet
la	**epidemia**	epidemic
la	**fiebre del heno**	hay fever
la	**insolación** (*pl* insolaciones)	sunstroke
la	**migraña**	migraine
la	**muleta**	crutch
la	**náusea**	nausea
la	**pandemia**	pandemic
las	**paperas**	mumps
la	**pomada**	ointment
la	**radiografía**	X-ray
la	**recuperación**	recovery
la	**rubeola**	German measles
la	**silla de ruedas**	wheelchair
la	**tos**	cough
la	**tos ferina**	whooping cough
la	**transfusión (de sangre)** (*pl* transfusiones (~ ~))	blood transfusion
la	**varicela**	chickenpox
la	**viruela**	smallpox

USEFUL PHRASES

gravemente herido(a) seriously injured
¿tiene seguro? are you insured?
estoy resfriado(a) I have a cold
¡eso duele! that hurts!; **me duele** it hurts!
respirar to breathe
desmayarse to faint
morir to die
perder el conocimiento to lose consciousness
llevar el brazo en cabestrillo to have one's arm in a sling

ESSENTIAL WORDS *(masculine)*

el	**almuerzo**	lunch
el	**ascensor**	lift
el	**balcón** *(pl balcones)*	balcony
los	**baños públicos** *(LAm)*	toilets
el	**bar**	bar
el	**camarero**	waiter
el	**cambio**	change
el	**cheque**	cheque
el	**cuarto de baño**	bathroom
el	**depósito**	deposit
el	**desayuno**	breakfast
el	**director**	manager
el	**equipaje**	luggage
el	**hotel**	hotel
el	**huésped**	guest
el	**impreso**	form
el	**maletero**	porter
el	**número**	number
el	**pasaporte**	passport
el	**piso**	floor; storey
el	**precio**	price
el	**recepcionista**	receptionist
el	**restaurante**	restaurant
el	**ruido**	noise
los	**servicios**	toilets
el	**teléfono**	telephone

USEFUL PHRASES

quisiera reservar una habitación I would like to book a room
una habitación con ducha/con baño a room with a shower/
 with a bathroom
una habitación individual a single room
una habitación doble a double room

ESSENTIAL WORDS *(feminine)*

la	**cama de matrimonio**	double bed
la	**camarera**	waitress
las	**camas separadas**	twin beds
la	**comida**	lunch; meal
la	**comodidad**	comfort
la	**cuenta**	bill
la	**directora**	manager
la	**ducha**	shower
la	**entrada**	entrance
la	**escalera**	stairs
la	**estancia**	stay
la	**fecha**	date
la	**ficha**	form
la	**habitación** (*pl* habitaciones)	room
la	**huésped**	guest
la	**llave**	key
la	**maleta**	suitcase
la	**media pensión**	half board
la	**noche**	night
la	**pensión** (*pl* pensiones)	guest house
la	**pensión completa**	full board
la	**piscina**	swimming pool
la	**planta**	floor; storey
la	**planta baja**	ground floor
la	**recepción**	reception
la	**recepcionista**	receptionist
la	**salida de incendios**	fire escape
la	**tarifa**	rate, rates
la	**televisión** (*pl* televisiones)	television
la	**vista**	view

USEFUL PHRASES

¿lleva algún documento de identidad? do you have any ID?
¿a qué hora se sirve el desayuno? what time is breakfast served?
limpiar la habitación to clean the room
"se ruega no molestar" "do not disturb"

IMPORTANT WORDS (*masculine*)

el	**albergue**	inn
el	**baño**	bathroom
el	**interruptor**	switch
el	**lavabo**	washbasin; bathroom
el	**precio total**	inclusive price
el	**recibo**	receipt

USEFUL WORDS (*masculine*)

el	**cocinero**	cook
el	**maître**	head waiter
el	**sumiller**	wine waiter
el	**vestíbulo**	foyer

USEFUL PHRASES

ocupado(a) occupied
libre vacant
limpio(a) clean
sucio(a) dirty
dormir to sleep
despertar to wake
"con todas las comodidades" "with all facilities"
¿podrían despertarme (*or* llamarme) mañana por la mañana a las siete?
  I'd like a 7 o'clock alarm call tomorrow morning, please
una habitación con vistas al mar a room overlooking the sea

IMPORTANT WORDS (feminine)

la	**bañera**	bathtub
la	**bienvenida**	welcome
la	**camarera (de habitaciones)**	chambermaid
la	**casa de huéspedes**	guest house
la	**factura**	bill
la	**guía turística**	guidebook
la	**propina**	tip
la	**reclamación** (pl reclamaciones)	complaint

USEFUL WORDS (feminine)

la	**cocinera**	cook

USEFUL PHRASES

una habitación con media pensión room with half board
¿nos sentamos fuera or **en la terraza?** shall we sit outside?
nos sirvieron la cena fuera or **en la terraza** we were served dinner outside
un hotel de tres estrellas a three-star hotel
IVA incluido inclusive of VAT

ESSENTIAL WORDS *(masculine)*

el	**aparcamiento** *(Sp)*	car park; parking space
el	**apartamento**	flat, apartment
el	**ascensor**	lift
el	**balcón** *(pl* balcones)	balcony
el	**bloque de departamentos** *(LAm)*	block of flats
el	**bloque de pisos** *(Sp)*	block of flats
el	**comedor**	dining room
el	**cuarto de baño**	bathroom
el	**departamento** *(LAm)*	flat, apartment
el	**dormitorio**	bedroom
el	**edificio**	building
el	**estacionamiento** *(LAm)*	car park; parking space
el	**exterior**	exterior
el	**garaje**	garage
el	**interior**	interior
el	**jardín** *(pl* jardines)	garden
el	**mueble**	piece of furniture
los	**muebles**	furniture
el	**numéro de teléfono**	phone number
el	**patio**	yard
el	**piso**	floor, storey; *(Sp)* flat, apartment
el	**pueblo**	village
el	**salón** *(pl* salones)	living room
el	**sótano**	basement
el	**terreno**	plot of land

USEFUL PHRASES

cuando vaya a casa when I go home
mirar por la ventana to look out of the window
en mi/tu/nuestra casa at my/your/our house
mudarse de casa to move house
alquilar un apartamento *or* **un piso** to rent a flat

ESSENTIAL WORDS (feminine)

la	**avenida**	avenue
la	**bodega**	cellar
la	**calefacción (central)**	(central) heating
	(pl calefacciones (~es))	
la	**calle**	street
la	**casa**	house
la	**ciudad**	town; city
la	**cocina**	kitchen
la	**comodidad**	comfort
la	**dirección** (pl direcciones)	address
la	**ducha**	shower
la	**entrada**	entrance
la	**entrada para coches** (Sp)	drive
	or **para carros** (LAm)	
la	**escalera**	stairs
la	**habitación** (pl habitaciones)	room
la	**llave**	key
la	**parcela**	plot of land
la	**pared**	wall
la	**planta**	floor, storey
la	**planta baja**	ground floor
la	**plaza de parking** or **de garaje**	parking space (in car park)
la	**puerta**	door
la	**puerta principal**	front door
la	**sala de estar**	living room
la	**urbanización** (pl urbanizaciones)	housing estate
la	**ventana**	window
la	**vista**	view

USEFUL PHRASES

vivo en una casa/en un apartamento or **un piso** I live in a house /a flat
(en el piso de) arriba upstairs
(en el piso de) abajo downstairs
en el primer piso on the first floor
en la planta baja on the ground floor
en casa at home

IMPORTANT WORDS (masculine)

el	**alojamiento**	accommodation
el	**alquiler**	rent
el	**baño**	toilet
el	**césped**	lawn
el	**dueño**	landlord; owner
el	**humo**	smoke
el	**lavabo**	toilet; washbasin
el	**mantenimiento**	upkeep
el	**mobiliario**	furniture
el	**pasillo**	corridor
el	**piso amueblado**	furnished flat
el	**portero**	caretaker
el	**propietario**	owner; landlord
el	**rellano**	landing
el	**tejado**	roof
el	**trastero**	lumber room; (*Mex*) cupboard
el	**vecino**	neighbour

USEFUL WORDS (masculine)

el	**ático**	penthouse; attic
el	**chalet** (*pl* ~s)	bungalow; detached house
el	**cristal**	window pane
el	**despacho**	study
el	**escalón** (*pl* escalones)	step
el	**estudio**	studio flat
el	**inquilino**	tenant; lodger
el	**muro**	wall
el	**parquet** (*pl* ~s)	parquet floor
el	**piso piloto**	show flat
el	**seto**	hedge
el	**suelo**	floor
el	**techo**	ceiling
el	**timbre**	door bell
el	**tragaluz** (*pl* tragaluces)	skylight
el	**umbral**	doorstep
el	**vestíbulo**	hall
el	**vidrio**	window pane

IMPORTANT WORDS (feminine)

la	**casa de campo**	cottage
la	**chimenea**	chimney; fireplace
la	**dueña**	landlady; owner
la	**mudanza**	move
la	**portera**	caretaker
la	**propietaria**	owner; landlady
la	**señora de la limpieza**	cleaner
la	**vecina**	neighbour
la	**vivienda**	housing

USEFUL WORDS (feminine)

el	**ama de casa** (f pl amas ~~)	housewife
la	**antena**	aerial
la	**baldosa**	tile
la	**buhardilla**	attic
la	**caldera**	boiler
la	**contraventana**	shutter
la	**cristalera** (Sp)	French window
la	**decoración** (pl decoraciones)	decoration
la	**fachada**	front (of house)
la	**habitación de los invitados**	spare room
la	**inquilina**	tenant; lodger
la	**persiana**	blind
la	**portería**	caretaker's room
la	**puerta ventana**	French window
la	**teja**	roof tile; slate
la	**tubería**	pipe
la	**vivienda de protección oficial**	council flat or house

USEFUL PHRASES

llamar a la puerta to knock at the door
acaba de sonar el timbre the doorbell's just gone
desde fuera from the outside
dentro on the inside
hasta el techo up to the ceiling

ESSENTIAL WORDS (*masculine*)

el	**armario**	cupboard; wardrobe
el	**bote de la basura** (*Mex*)	dustbin
el	**buzón** (*pl* buzones)	letterbox
el	**cazo**	saucepan
el	**cenicero**	ashtray
el	**cepillo**	brush
el	**cuadro**	picture
el	**cubo de la basura**	dustbin
el	**despertador**	alarm clock
el	**espejo**	mirror
el	**fregadero**	sink
el	**frigorífico** (*Sp*)	fridge
el	**gas**	gas
el	**grifo**	tap
el	**interruptor**	switch
el	**jabón** (*pl* jabones)	soap
el	**lavabo**	washbasin; toilet
la	**pasta de dientes**	toothpaste
el	**póster** (*pl* ~es *or* ~s)	poster
el	**radiador**	radiator
el	**refrigerador** (*LAm*)	fridge
el	**televisor**	television set
el	**vídeo** (*Sp*) *or* **video** (*LAm*)	video recorder

USEFUL PHRASES
darse un baño, bañarse to have a bath
darse una ducha, ducharse to have a shower
hacer la limpieza de la casa to do the housework
me gusta cocinar I like cooking

ESSENTIAL WORDS *(feminine)*

el	**agua** *(f)*	water
la	**alfombra**	carpet, rug
la	**almohada**	pillow
la	**balanza**	scales
la	**bandeja**	tray
la	**bañera**	bath
la	**cacerola**	saucepan
la	**cafetera**	coffee pot; coffee maker
la	**cazuela**	saucepan
la	**cocina**	cooker
las	**cortinas**	curtains
la	**ducha**	shower
la	**electricidad**	electricity
la	**foto**	photo
la	**lámpara**	lamp
la	**lavadora**	washing machine
la	**luz** *(pl* luces*)*	light
la	**manta**	blanket
la	**radio**	radio
la	**refrigeradora** *(LAm)*	fridge
la	**sábana**	sheet
la	**servilleta**	napkin
las	**tareas domésticas**	housework
la	**televisión** *(pl* televisiones*)*	television
la	**toalla**	towel
la	**vajilla**	dishes

USEFUL PHRASES
ver la televisión to watch television
en televisión on television
encender/apagar la tele to switch on/off the TV
tirar algo al cubo de la basura to throw sth in the dustbin
lavar *or* **fregar los platos** to do the dishes

IMPORTANT WORDS (*masculine*)

el	**bidé**	bidet
el	**detergente (en polvo)**	washing powder
el	**enchufe**	plug; socket
el	**horno**	oven
el	**lavavajillas** (*pl inv*)	dishwasher; washing-up liquid
el	**mueble de cocina**	cooker
el	**polvo**	dust

USEFUL WORDS (*masculine*)

el	**adorno**	ornament
el	**almohadón** (*pl* almohadones)	bolster
el	**cojín** (*pl* cojines)	cushion
el	**cubo**	bucket
el	**edredón nórdico** (*pl* edredones ~s)	duvet
el	**horno microondas**	microwave oven
el	**jarrón** (*pl* jarrones)	vase
el	**molinillo de café**	coffee grinder
el	**paño de cocina**	dishcloth
el	**papel pintado**	wallpaper
el	**picaporte**	door handle
el	**trapo (del polvo)**	duster

USEFUL PHRASES
enchufar/desenchufar to plug in/to unplug
pasar la aspiradora to hoover
hacer la colada to do the washing

IMPORTANT WORDS (feminine)

la	aspiradora	vacuum cleaner
la	bombilla	light bulb
la	cerradura	lock
la	colada	(clean) washing
la	estufa	heater
la	pintura	paint; painting
la	receta	recipe
la	ropa de cama	bedclothes
la	ropa sucia	(dirty) washing, laundry
la	sartén (pl sartenes)	frying pan
la	señora de la limpieza	cleaner

USEFUL WORDS (feminine)

la	basura	rubbish
la	batidora	blender
la	bayeta	duster
la	escalera (de mano)	ladder
la	escoba	broom
la	esponja	sponge
la	manta eléctrica	electric blanket
la	moqueta	fitted carpet
la	olla a presión	pressure cooker
la	papelera	waste paper basket
la	percha	coat hanger
la	plancha	iron
la	tabla de planchar	ironing board
la	tapa	lid
la	tapicería	upholstery
la	tostadora	toaster

USEFUL PHRASES

barrer to sweep (up)
limpiar to clean
recoger uno sus cosas to tidy away one's things
dejar uno sus cosas por ahí tiradas to leave one's things lying about

ESSENTIAL WORDS *(masculine)*

el **banco**	bank
el **billete (de banco)**	banknote
el **bolígrafo**	Biro®
el **buzón** *(pl buzones)*	postbox
el **cambio**	change
el **carnet** *or* **carné de identidad** *(Sp)* *(pl ~s ~~)*	ID card
el **cartero**	postman
el **céntimo de euro**	euro cent
el **cheque**	cheque
el **código postal**	postcode
el **contrato telefónico**	phone contract
el **correo electrónico**	email
el **documento de identidad**	ID card
el **empleado**	counter clerk
el **error**	mistake
el **euro**	euro
el **fax**	fax; fax machine
el **impreso**	form
el **ingreso**	deposit
el **justificante**	written proof
el **mensaje de texto**	text message
el **mostrador**	counter
el **prefijo**	dialling code
el **número**	number
el **paquete**	parcel
el **pasaporte**	passport
el **precio**	price
el **sello**	stamp
el **sobre**	envelope
el **teléfono**	telephone
el **tono de marcado**	dialling tone

USEFUL PHRASES

el banco más cercano the nearest bank
quisiera cobrar un cheque/cambiar dinero I would like to cash a
  cheque/change some money

ESSENTIAL WORDS *(feminine)*

la	**caja**	check-out
la	**carta**	letter
la	**cartera**	postwoman; wallet; (*LAm*) handbag
la	**cédula de identidad** (*LAm*)	ID card
la	**compañía de teléfonos**	phone company
la	**dirección** (*pl* direcciones)	address
la	**empleada**	counter clerk
la	**firma**	signature
la	**información**	information; directory enquiries
la	**libra (esterlina)**	pound (sterling)
la	**llamada**	call
la	**oficina de correos**	post office
la	**oficina de información y turismo**	tourist information office
la	**pluma**	pen
la	**respuesta**	reply
la	**tarjeta de crédito**	credit card
la	**tarjeta de débito**	debit card
la	**(tarjeta) postal**	postcard

USEFUL PHRASES

una llamada telefónica a phone call
llamar a algn por teléfono, telefonear a algn to phone sb
descolgar el teléfono to lift the receiver
marcar (el número) to dial (the number)
hola – soy el Dr Pérez *or* **el Dr Pérez al habla** hello, this is Dr. Pérez
la línea está ocupada the line is engaged
no cuelgue hold the line
me he equivocado de número I got the wrong number
colgar to hang up
quisiera hacer una llamada internacional I'd like to make an international phone call

IMPORTANT WORDS *(masculine)*

el **archivo adjunto**	attachment
el **buzón de voz** *(pl* buzones ~~ *)*	voicemail
el **cheque de viaje**	traveller's cheque
el **cibercafé**	internet café
el **contestador (automático)**	answerphone
el **correo**	mail
el **crédito**	credit
el **domicilio**	home address
el **gasto**	expense
el **impuesto**	tax
el **monedero**	purse
el **pago**	payment
el **papel de carta**	writing paper
el **recargo**	extra charge
el **SMS** *(pl inv)*	text message
el **talonario de cheques**	cheque book
el **telefonista**	operator
el **(teléfono) fijo**	landline
el **(teléfono) móvil**	mobile (phone)
el **telegrama**	telegram
el **tipo de cambio**	exchange rate

USEFUL WORDS *(masculine)*

el **apartado de correos**	PO box
el **auricular**	receiver
el **destinatario**	addressee
el **documento adjunto**	attachment
el **giro postal**	postal order
el **nombre de acceso (***or* **entrada) al sistema**	login
el **papel de envolver**	wrapping paper
el **remitente**	sender
el **tono de llamada**	ringtone

IMPORTANT WORDS (feminine)

la	**banda ancha**	broadband
la	**cabina telefónica**	callbox
la	**contraseña**	password
la	**cuenta (bancaria)**	(bank) account
la	**estampilla**	stamp
la	**guía telefónica**	telephone directory
la	**llamada telefónica**	phone call
la	**oficina de objetos perdidos**	lost property office
la	**ranura**	slot
la	**recogida**	collection
la	**recompensa**	reward
la	**tarjeta telefónica**	(*prepaid*) phonecard
la	**tarjeta de recarga (del móvil)**	top-up (card)
la	**telefonista**	operator

USEFUL WORDS (feminine)

la	**carta certificada**	registered letter
la	**destinataria**	addressee
la	**llamada internacional**	international call
la	**llamada local**	local call
la	**llamada nacional**	inter-city call
la	**oficina de cambio**	bureau de change
la	**remitente**	sender
la	**tarjeta SIM** (*pl* ~s ~)	SIM card

USEFUL PHRASES

he perdido la cartera I've lost my wallet
rellenar un impreso to fill in a form
en mayúsculas in block letters
hacer una llamada a cobro revertido to make a reverse charge call

GENERAL SITUATIONS

¿cuál es su dirección? what is your address?
¿cómo se escribe? how do you spell that?
¿tiene cambio de 100 euros? do you have change of 100 euros?
escribir to write
responder to reply
firmar to sign
¿me puede ayudar por favor? can you help me please?
¿cómo se va a la estación? how do I get to the station?
todo recto straight on
a la derecha to *or* on the right; **a la izquierda** to *or* on the left

LETTERS

Querido Carlos Dear Carlos
Querida Ana Dear Ana
Estimado señor Dear Sir
Estimada señora Dear Madam
recuerdos, saludos best wishes
un abrazo de, un beso de, besos de love from
le saluda atentamente *or* **cordialmente** kind regards
besos y abrazos love and kisses
atentamente yours faithfully
reciba un atento saludo, le saluda atentamente yours sincerely
sigue PTO

EMAILS

mandarle un correo electrónico a algn to mail *or* email sb

MOBILES

mandarle un mensaje de texto a algn to text sb

PRONUNCIATION GUIDE

Pronounced approximately as:

A	ah
B	bay
C	thay, say
D	day
E	ay
F	efay
G	khay
H	atchay
I	ee
J	khota
K	kah
L	elay
LL	elyay
M	emay
N	enay
Ñ	enyay
O	oh
P	pay
Q	koo
R	eray
S	essay
T	tay
U	oo
V	oobay (*Sp*), **bay korta** (*LAm*)
W	oobay doblay (*Sp*), **doblay bay** (*LAm*)
X	ekees
Y	ee griayga
Z	theta, seta

ESSENTIAL WORDS (*masculine*)

el **abogado**	lawyer
el **accidente**	accident
el **carnet de identidad** (*Sp*) (*pl* ~s ~ ~)	ID card
el **documento de identidad**	ID card
el **incendio**	fire
el **policía**	policeman
el **problema**	problem
el **robo**	burglary; theft

IMPORTANT WORDS (*masculine*)

el **atracador**	armed robber; mugger
el **atraco**	hold-up; mugging
el **consulado**	consulate
el **control policial**	checkpoint; roadblock
el **culpable**	culprit
el **daño** *or* **los daños**	damage
el **ejército**	army
el **espía**	spy
el **gobierno**	government
el **guardia civil**	civil guard (*person*)
los **impuestos**	income tax
el **ladrón** (*pl* ladrones)	burglar; thief; robber
el **monedero**	purse
el **muerto**	dead man
el **permiso**	permission
el **propietario**	owner
el **testigo**	witness

USEFUL PHRASES

robar to burgle; to steal; to rob
¡me han robado la cartera! someone has stolen my wallet!
ilegal illegal; **inocente** innocent
no es culpa mía it's not my fault
¡socorro! help!; **¡al ladrón!** stop thief!
¡fuego! fire!; **¡arriba las manos!** hands up!
robar un banco to rob a bank
encarcelar to imprison; **fugarse, escapar** to escape

ESSENTIAL WORDS *(feminine)*

la	**abogada**	lawyer
la	**cédula de identidad** *(LAm)*	identity card
la	**culpa**	fault
la	**documentación**	papers
la	**identidad**	identity
la	**policía**	police; policewoman
la	**verdad**	truth

IMPORTANT WORDS *(feminine)*

la	**atracadora**	armed robber; mugger
la	**banda**	gang
la	**cartera**	wallet; *(LAm)* handbag
la	**comisaría**	police station
la	**culpable**	culprit
la	**denuncia**	report
la	**espía**	spy
la	**Guardia Civil**	Civil Guard
la	**guardia civil**	civil guard *(person)*
la	**ladrona**	burglar; thief; robber
la	**manifestación** *(pl* manifestaciones*)*	demonstration
la	**muerta**	dead woman
la	**muerte**	death
la	**multa**	fine
la	**pena de muerte**	death penalty
la	**póliza de seguros**	insurance policy
la	**propietaria**	owner
la	**recompensa**	reward
la	**testigo**	witness

USEFUL PHRASES

un atraco a mano armada a hold-up
raptar *or* **secuestrar a un niño** to abduct a child
un grupo de gamberros a bunch of hooligans
en la cárcel in prison
pelearse to fight; **arrestar** to arrest; **acusar** to charge
estar detenido(a) to be remanded in custody
acusar a algn de algo to accuse sb of sth; to charge sb with sth

USEFUL WORDS (*masculine*)

el	arresto	arrest
el	asesinato	murder
el	asesino	murderer
el	botín (*pl* botines)	loot
el	cadáver	corpse
el	crimen (*pl* crímenes)	murder; crime
el	criminal	criminal
el	detective privado	private detective
el	disparo (de arma)	(gun) shot
el	drogadicto	drug addict
el	encarcelamiento	imprisonment
el	estafador	crook
el	gamberro	hooligan
el	gángster (*pl* ~s)	gangster
el	guarda	guard; warden
el	guardia	guard; policeman
el	inmigrante ilegal	illegal immigrant
el	intento	attempt
el	juez (*pl* jueces)	judge
el	juicio	trial
el	jurado	jury
el	levantamiento	uprising
el	pirómano	arsonist
el	poli	cop
el	preso	prisoner
el	rehén (*pl* rehenes)	hostage
el	rescate	ransom; rescue
el	revólver	revolver
el	secuestrador	kidnapper; hijacker
el	secuestro	kidnapping
el	secuestro aéreo	hijacking
el	terrorismo	terrorism
el	terrorista	terrorist
el	traficante de drogas	drug dealer
el	tribunal	court
los	tribunales	law courts
el	valor	bravery

USEFUL WORDS *(feminine)*

la	**acusación** *(pl* acusaciones)	the prosecution; charge
el	**arma** *(pl f* las **armas**)	weapon
la	**asesina**	murderer
la	**bomba**	bomb
la	**cárcel**	prison
la	**celda**	cell
la	**criminal**	criminal
la	**declaración** *(pl* declaraciones)	statement
la	**defensa**	defence
la	**detective privada**	private detective
la	**detención** *(pl* detenciones)	arrest
la	**droga**	drug
la	**drogadicta**	drug addict
la	**estafadora**	crook
la	**fuga**	escape
la	**gamberra**	hooligan
la	**guarda**	guard; warden
la	**guardia**	guard; policewoman
la	**inmigrante ilegal**	illegal immigrant
la	**investigación** *(pl* investigaciones)	inquiry
la	**ley**	law
la	**multa**	fine
la	**pelea**	fight
la	**pirómana**	arsonist
la	**pistola**	gun
la	**poli**	the cops; cop
la	**prisión** *(pl* prisiones)	prison
la	**presa**	prisoner
la	**prueba**	proof
las	**pruebas**	evidence
la	**redada**	raid
la	**rehén** *(pl* rehenes)	hostage
la	**riña**	argument
la	**secuestradora**	kidnapper; hijacker
la	**suplantación de personalidad** *(pl* suplantaciones ~ ~)	identity theft
la	**terrorista**	terrorist
la	**traficante de drogas**	drug dealer

ESSENTIAL WORDS (*masculine*)

el	**acero**	steel
el	**algodón**	cotton
el	**caucho**	rubber
el	**cristal**	glass
el	**cuero**	leather
el	**gas**	gas
el	**gasoil**	diesel
el	**hierro**	iron
el	**metal**	metal
el	**oro**	gold
el	**plástico**	plastic
el	**vidrio**	glass

IMPORTANT WORDS (*masculine*)

el	**acero inoxidable**	stainless steel
el	**aluminio**	aluminium
el	**cartón**	cardboard
el	**estado**	condition
el	**hierro forjado**	wrought iron
el	**ladrillo**	brick
el	**papel**	paper
el	**tejido**	fabric

USEFUL PHRASES

una silla de madera a wooden chair
una caja de plástico a plastic box
un anillo de oro a gold ring
en buen estado, en buenas condiciones in good condition
en mal estado, en malas condiciones in bad condition

ESSENTIAL WORDS (feminine)

la	**lana**	wool
la	**madera**	wood
la	**piedra**	stone
la	**piel**	fur; leather
la	**plata**	silver
la	**tela**	fabric

IMPORTANT WORDS (feminine)

la	**fibra sintética**	synthetic fibre
la	**seda**	silk

USEFUL PHRASES
un abrigo de piel a fur coat
un jersey de lana a woollen jumper
oxidado(a) rusty

USEFUL WORDS *(masculine)*

el **acrílico**	acrylic
el **alambre**	wire
el **ante**	suede
el **bronce**	bronze
el **carbón**	coal
el **cemento**	concrete
el **cobre**	copper
el **encaje**	lace
el **estaño**	tin
el **hilo**	thread
el **latón**	brass
el **lino**	linen
el **líquido**	liquid
el **mármol**	marble
el **material**	material
el **mimbre**	wickerwork
el **pegamento**	glue
el **plomo**	lead
el **raso**	satin
el **terciopelo**	velvet
el **tweed**	tweed

USEFUL WORDS *(feminine)*

la	arcilla	clay
la	cera	wax
la	cerámica	ceramics
la	cola	glue
la	cuerda	string
la	escayola	plaster
la	gomaespuma	foam rubber
la	hojalata	tin, tinplate
la	lona	canvas
la	loza	pottery
la	paja	straw
la	pana	corduroy
la	porcelana	china

ESSENTIAL WORDS (*masculine*)

el	**director de orquesta**	conductor
el	**grupo**	band
el	**instrumento musical**	musical instrument
el	**músico**	musician
el	**piano**	piano
el	**violín** (*pl* violines)	violin

USEFUL WORDS (*masculine*)

el	**acorde**	chord
el	**acordeón** (*pl* acordeones)	accordion
el	**arco**	bow
el	**atril**	music stand
el	**bombo**	bass drum
el	**clarinete**	clarinet
el	**contrabajo**	double bass
el	**estuche**	case
el	**estudio de grabación**	recording studio
el	**fagot**	bassoon
los	**instrumentos de cuerda**	string instruments
los	**instrumentos de percusión**	percussion instruments
los	**instrumentos de viento**	wind instruments
el	**jazz**	jazz
los	**metales**	brass
el	**micrófono**	microphone
el	**minidisco**	minidisc
el	**oboe**	oboe
el	**órgano**	organ
los	**platillos**	cymbals
el	**saxofón** (*pl* saxofones)	saxophone
el	**solfeo**	music theory
el	**solista**	soloist
el	**tambor**	drum
el	**triángulo**	triangle
el	**trombón** (*pl* trombones)	trombone
el	**violonchelo**	cello

ESSENTIAL WORDS *(feminine)*

la	**batería**	drums, drum kit
la	**directora de orquesta**	conductor
la	**flauta**	flute
la	**flauta dulce**	recorder
la	**guitarra**	guitar
la	**música**	music; musician
la	**orquesta**	orchestra

USEFUL WORDS *(feminine)*

la	**armónica**	harmonica
el	**arpa**	harpe
la	**batuta**	conductor's baton
la	**composición** *(pl* composiciones)	composition
la	**corneta**	bugle
la	**cuerda**	string
la	**gaita**	bagpipes
la	**grabación digital** *(pl* grabaciones ~es)	digital recording
la	**megafonía**	PA system
la	**mesa de mezclas**	mixing deck
la	**nota**	note
la	**pandereta**	tambourine
la	**solista**	soloist
la	**tecla (de piano)**	(piano) key
la	**trompeta**	trumpet
la	**viola**	viola

USEFUL PHRASES

tocar *or* **interpretar una pieza** to play a piece
tocar alto/bajo to play loudly/softly
tocar afinado/desafinado to play in tune/out of tune
tocar el piano/la guitarra to play the piano/the guitar
tocar la batería to play drums
Pedro a la batería Pedro on drums
practicar el piano to practise the piano
¿tocas en un grupo? do you play in a band?
una nota falsa a wrong note

CARDINAL NUMBERS

cero	0	zero
uno (*m*), una (*f*)	1	one
dos	2	two
tres	3	three
cuatro	4	four
cinco	5	five
seis	6	six
siete	7	seven
ocho	8	eight
nueve	9	nine
diez	10	ten
once	11	eleven
doce	12	twelve
trece	13	thirteen
catorce	14	fourteen
quince	15	fifteen
dieciséis	16	sixteen
diecisiete	17	seventeen
dieciocho	18	eighteen
diecinueve	19	nineteen
veinte	20	twenty
veintiuno(a)	21	twenty-one
veintidós	22	twenty-two
veintitrés	23	twenty-three
treinta	30	thirty
treinta y uno(a)	31	thirty-one
treinta y dos	32	thirty-two
cuarenta	40	forty
cincuenta	50	fifty
sesenta	60	sixty
setenta	70	seventy
ochenta	80	eighty
noventa	90	ninety
cien	100	one hundred

CARDINAL NUMBERS *(continued)*

ciento uno(a)	101	a hundred and one
ciento dos	102	a hundred and two
ciento diez	110	a hundred and ten
ciento ochenta y dos	182	a hundred and eighty-two
doscientos(as)	200	two hundred
doscientos(as) uno(a)	201	two hundred and one
doscientos(as) dos	202	two hundred and two
trescientos(as)	300	three hundred
cuatrocientos(as)	400	four hundred
quinientos(as)	500	five hundred
seiscientos(as)	600	six hundred
setecientos(as)	700	seven hundred
ochocientos(as)	800	eight hundred
novecientos(as)	900	nine hundred
mil	1000	one thousand
mil uno(a)	1001	a thousand and one
mil dos	1002	a thousand and two
dos mil	2000	two thousand
dos mil seis	2006	two thousand and six
diez mil	10000	ten thousand
cien mil	100000	one hundred thousand
un millón	1000000	one million
dos millones	2000000	two million

USEFUL PHRASES
mil euros a thousand euros
un millón de dólares one million dollars
tres coma dos (3,2) three point two (3.2)

ORDINAL NUMBERS

primero(a)	1º, 1ª	first
segundo(a)	2º, 2ª	second
tercero(a)	3º, 3ª	third
cuarto(a)	4º, 4ª	fourth
quinto(a)	5º, 5ª	fifth
sexto(a)	6º, 6ª	sixth
séptimo(a)	7º, 7ª	seventh
octavo(a)	8º, 8ª	eighth
noveno(a)	9º, 9ª	ninth
décimo(a)	10º, 10ª	tenth
undécimo(a)	11º, 11ª	eleventh
duodécimo(a)	12º, 12ª	twelfth
decimotercero(a)	13º, 13ª	thirteenth
decimocuarto(a)	14º, 14ª	fourteenth
decimoquinto(a)	15º, 15ª	fifteenth
decimosexto(a)	16º, 16ª	sixteenth
decimoséptimo(a)	17º, 17ª	seventeenth
decimoctavo(a)	18º, 18ª	eighteenth
decimonoveno(a), decimonono(a)	19º, 19ª	nineteenth
vigésimo(a)	20º, 20ª	twentieth

Note:

Ordinal numbers are hardly ever used above 10th in spoken Spanish, and rarely at all above 20th. It's normal to use the cardinal numbers instead, except for **milésimo(a)**.

milésimo(a)	1000º, 1000ª	thousandth
dos milésimo(a)	2000º, 2000ª	two thousandth
millonésimo(a)	1000000º, 1000000ª	millionth
dos millonésimo(a)	2000000º, 2000000ª	two millionth

FRACTIONS

un medio	$\frac{1}{2}$	a half
uno(a) y medio(a)	$1\frac{1}{2}$	one and a half
dos y medio(a)	$2\frac{1}{2}$	two and a half
un tercio, la tercera parte	$\frac{1}{3}$	a third
dos tercios, las dos terceras partes	$\frac{2}{3}$	two thirds
un cuarto, la cuarta parte	$\frac{1}{4}$	a quarter
tres cuartos, las tres cuartas partes	$\frac{3}{4}$	three quarters
un sexto, la sexta parte	$\frac{1}{6}$	a sixth
tres y cinco sextos	$3\frac{5}{6}$	three and five sixths
un séptimo, la séptima parte	$\frac{1}{7}$	a seventh
un octavo, la octava parte	$\frac{1}{8}$	an eighth
un noveno, la novena parte	$\frac{1}{9}$	a ninth
un décimo, la décima parte	$\frac{1}{10}$	a tenth
un onceavo, la onceava parte	$\frac{1}{11}$	an eleventh
un doceavo, la doceava parte	$\frac{1}{12}$	a twelfth
siete doceavos, las siete doceavas partes	$\frac{7}{12}$	seven twelfths
un centésimo, la centésima parte	$\frac{1}{100}$	a hundredth
un milésimo, la milésima parte	$\frac{1}{1000}$	a thousandth

USEFUL PHRASES

ambos (*f* ambas), los dos (*f* las dos) both of them
un bocado de a mouthful of
un bote de a jar of; a tin *or* can of
una botella de a bottle of
un botellín (de cerveza) a small bottle (of beer)
una caja de a box of
(gran) cantidad de lots of
una caña (de cerveza) a small glass of beer
cien gramos de a hundred grammes of
un centenar de (about) a hundred
un cuarto de a quarter of
tres cuartos de three quarters of
una cucharada de a spoonful of
una docena de (about) a dozen
un grupo de a group of
una jarra de a jug of; a mug of (*beer*)
un kilo de a kilo of
un litro de a litre of
la mayoría (de), la mayor parte (de) most (of)
media docena de half a dozen
medio litro de half a litre of
una loncha de jamón a slice of ham
un metro de a metre of
miles de thousands of

USEFUL PHRASES

la mitad de half of
un montón de a pile of
mucho(a) a lot of, much
muchos (*f* muchas) a lot of, many
multitud de, montones de loads of
un paquete de a packet of
un par de a pair of
un plato de a plate of
un poco de a little; some
una porción de a portion of
un puñado de a handful of
una rebanada de pan a slice of bread
un rebaño de a herd of (*cattle*); a flock of (*sheep*)
una rodaja de merluza a slice of hake
un sobre de sopa a packet of soup
una taza de a cup of
un tazón de a bowl of
un terrón de azúcar a lump of sugar
un tonel de a barrel of
un trozo de papel/pastel a piece of paper/cake
a unos metros de a few metres from
un vaso de a glass of
varios several
a varios kilómetros de a few kilometres from

ESSENTIAL WORDS *(masculine)*

el	**anillo**	ring
el	**cepillo**	brush
el	**cepillo de dientes**	toothbrush
el	**champú**	shampoo
el	**desodorante**	deodorant
el	**espejo**	mirror
el	**maquillaje**	make-up
el	**peine**	comb
el	**perfume**	perfume
el	**reloj**	watch

USEFUL WORDS *(masculine)*

el	**aftershave**	aftershave
el	**broche**	brooch
el	**colgante**	pendant
el	**collar**	necklace
el	**dentífrico**	toothpaste
el	**diamante**	diamond
los	**efectos personales**	personal effects
el	**esmalte (de uñas)**	nail varnish
el	**gemelo**	cufflink
el	**kleenex®** *(pl inv)*	tissue
el	**lápiz de labios** *(pl lápices ~ ~)*	lipstick
el	**llavero**	key-ring
el	**maquillaje**	make-up
el	**neceser**	toilet bag
el	**papel higiénico**	toilet paper
el	**peinado**	hairstyle
el	**pendiente**	earring
los	**polvos compactos**	face powder
los	**polvos para la cara**	face powder
el	**quitaesmalte**	nail varnish remover
el	**rímel**	mascara
el	**rulo**	roller
el	**secador**	hairdryer

ESSENTIAL WORDS (feminine)

el	**agua de colonia** (f)	eau de toilette
la	**cadena**	chain
la	**crema para la cara**	face cream
la	**cuchilla de afeitar**	razor
la	**joya**	jewel
la	**maquinilla de afeitar**	(safety) razor
la	**pasta de dientes**	toothpaste
la	**pulsera**	bracelet

USEFUL WORDS (feminine)

la	**alianza**	wedding ring
la	**base de maquillaje**	foundation
la	**brocha de afeitar**	shaving brush
la	**crema de afeitar**	shaving cream
la	**esponja**	sponge
la	**espuma de afeitar**	shaving foam
la	**manicura**	manicure
la	**perla**	pearl
la	**polvera**	(powder) compact
la	**sombra de ojos**	eye shadow

USEFUL PHRASES

maquillarse to put on one's make-up
desmaquillarse to take off one's make-up
hacerse un peinado to do one's hair
peinarse to comb one's hair
cepillarse el pelo to brush one's hair
afeitarse to shave
lavarse los dientes, limpiarse los dientes to clean or brush one's teeth

ESSENTIAL WORDS (*masculine*)

el	**árbol**	tree
el	**césped**	lawn
el	**jardín** (*pl* jardines)	garden
el	**jardinero**	gardener
el	**sol**	sun

IMPORTANT WORDS (*masculine*)

el	**arbusto**	bush
el	**banco**	bench
el	**camino**	path
el	**cultivo**	cultivation; crop
el	**ramo de flores**	bunch of flowers

USEFUL PHRASES

plantar to plant
quitar las malas hierbas, desherbar to weed
regalar a algn un ramo de flores to give sb a bunch of flowers
cortar el césped to mow the lawn
"no pisar el césped" "keep off the grass"
a mi padre le gusta la jardinería my father likes gardening

ESSENTIAL WORDS (feminine)

la	flor	flower
la	hierba	grass
la	hoja	leaf
la	jardinera	gardener; flower bed
la	jardinería	gardening
la	lluvia	rain
la	planta	plant
la	rama	branch
la	rosa	rose
la	tierra	land; soil; ground
las	verduras	vegetables

IMPORTANT WORDS (feminine)

la	abeja	bee
la	avispa	wasp
las	malas hierbas	weeds
la	raíz (pl. raíces)	root
la	sombra	shade; shadow
la	valla	fence
la	verja	gate

USEFUL PHRASES

las flores están creciendo the flowers are growing
en el suelo on the ground
regar las plantas to water the flowers
coger flores to pick flowers
irse a la sombra to go into the shade
quedarse en la sombra to remain in the shade
a la sombra de un árbol in the shade of a tree

USEFUL WORDS (*masculine*)

el	**arriate**	flowerbed
el	**azafrán** (*pl* azafranes)	crocus
el	**brote**	bud
el	**clavel**	carnation
el	**cortacésped**	lawnmower
el	**crisantemo**	chrysanthemum
el	**diente de león**	dandelion
el	**estanque**	(ornamental) pool
el	**follaje**	leaves
el	**girasol**	sunflower
el	**gusano**	worm
el	**huerto**	vegetable garden
el	**invernadero**	greenhouse
el	**invierno**	winter
el	**jacinto**	hyacinth
el	**lirio**	lily
el	**lirio del valle**	lily of the valley
el	**narciso**	daffodil
el	**otoño**	autumn, fall
el	**parterre**	flowerbed
el	**pensamiento**	pansy
el	**ranúnculo**	buttercup
el	**rocío**	dew
el	**rosal**	rose bush
el	**sendero**	path
el	**seto**	hedge
el	**suelo**	ground; soil
el	**tallo**	stalk
el	**tronco**	trunk (*of tree*)
el	**tulipán** (*pl* tulipanes)	tulip
el	**verano**	summer

USEFUL WORDS *(feminine)*

la	**amapola**	poppy
la	**baya**	berry
la	**campanilla**	campanula, bellflower
la	**campanilla de invierno**	snowdrop
la	**carretilla**	wheelbarrow
la	**cerca**	fence
la	**cosecha**	crop
la	**espina**	thorn
la	**herramienta**	tool
la	**hiedra**	ivy
la	**hortensia**	hydrangea
las	**lilas**	lilac
la	**madreselva**	honeysuckle
la	**manguera**	hose
la	**margarita**	daisy
la	**mariposa**	butterfly
la	**orquídea**	orchid
la	**peonía**	peony
la	**primavera**	spring; primrose
la	**regadera**	watering can
la	**semilla**	seed
la	**violeta**	violet

ESSENTIAL WORDS (*masculine*)

los	**anteojos de sol** (*LAm*)	sunglasses
el	**bañador**	swimming trunks; swimsuit
el	**bañista**	swimmer
el	**barco**	boat; ship
el	**barco de pesca**	fishing boat
el	**bikini**	bikini
el	**bote**	boat
el	**mar**	sea
el	**muelle**	quay
el	**paseo**	walk
el	**pescador**	fisherman
el	**pesquero**	fishing boat
el	**picnic** (*pl* ~s)	picnic
el	**puerto**	port, harbour
el	**puerto deportivo**	marina
el	**remo**	rowing; oar
el	**traje de baño**	swimming trunks; swimsuit

IMPORTANT WORDS (*masculine*)

el	**cangrejo**	crab
el	**castillo de arena**	sandcastle
el	**fondo**	bottom
el	**horizonte**	horizon
el	**mareo**	seasickness
el	**veraneante**	holiday-maker

USEFUL PHRASES

en la playa at the seaside; at *or* on the beach
en el horizonte on the horizon
está mareado he is seasick
nadar to swim
ahogarse to drown
me voy a dar un baño I'm going for a swim
tirarse al agua, zambullirse to dive into the water
flotar to float

ESSENTIAL WORDS (feminine)

el	**agua** (f)	water
la	**arena**	sand
la	**bañista**	swimmer
la	**barca**	boat
la	**costa**	coast
las	**gafas de sol** (Sp)	sunglasses
la	**isla**	island
la	**natación**	swimming
la	**pescadora**	fisherwoman
la	**piedra**	stone
la	**playa**	beach; seaside
las	**quemaduras de sol**	sunburn
la	**toalla**	towel

IMPORTANT WORDS (feminine)

la	**colchoneta inflable**	airbed, lilo®
la	**crema (de protección) solar**	suncream
la	**tabla de windsurf**	windsurfing board
la	**travesía**	crossing
la	**tumbona**	deckchair
la	**veraneante**	holiday-maker

USEFUL PHRASES

en el fondo del mar at the bottom of the sea
hacer la travesía en barco to go across by boat
broncearse, ponerse moreno(a) to get a tan
estar moreno(a) to be tanned
sabe nadar he can swim

USEFUL WORDS *(masculine)*

el	acantilado	cliff
el	aire de mar	sea air
el	balde	bucket
el	(barco de) vapor	steamer
los	binoculares	binoculars
el	bote de pedales	pedalo
el	cabo	headland
el	crucero	cruise
el	cubo	bucket
el	embarcadero	pier
el	estuario	estuary
el	faro	lighthouse
el	guijarro	pebble
el	marinero	sailor
el	marino	sailor; naval officer
el	mástil	mast
el	naufragio	shipwreck
los	náufragos	shipwrecked people, castaways
el	océano	ocean
el	oleaje	swell
el	pedal *(Sp)*	pedalo
los	prismáticos	binoculars
el	puente (de mando)	bridge *(of ship)*
los	restos de un naufragio	wreckage
el	salvavidas *(pl inv)*	lifeguard; lifebelt
el	socorrista	lifeguard
el	timón *(pl timones)*	rudder
el	transbordador	ferry

USEFUL WORDS (feminine)

las	**algas**	seaweed
el	**ancla** (pl f las **anclas**)	anchor
la	**bahía**	bay
la	**balsa**	raft
la	**bandera**	flag
la	**barca**	small boat
la	**boya**	buoy
la	**brisa marina**	sea breeze
la	**carga**	cargo
la	**concha**	shell
la	**corriente**	current
la	**desembocadura**	mouth (of river)
la	**espuma**	foam
la	**gaviota**	seagull
la	**insolación** (pl insolaciones)	sunstroke
la	**marea**	tide
la	**marina**	navy
la	**marinera**	sailor
la	**marina**	sailor; naval officer
la	**nave**	vessel
la	**ola**	wave
la	**orilla**	shore
la	**pala**	spade
la	**pasarela**	gangway
la	**ría**	estuary
la	**roca**	rock
la	**salvavidas** (pl inv) or **socorrista**	lifeguard
la	**sombrilla**	parasol
la	**tripulación** (pl tripulaciones)	crew
la	**vela**	sail; sailing

USEFUL PHRASES

tuve una insolación I had sunstroke
con la marea baja/alta at low/high tide
hacer vela to go sailing

ESSENTIAL WORDS (masculine)

el	banco	bank
el	billete (de banco)	banknote
el	cambio	change
el	céntimo	cent
el	centro comercial	shopping centre
el	cheque	cheque
el	cliente	customer
el	departamento	department
el	dependiente	shop assistant, sales assistant
el	descuento	discount
el	dinero	money
el	estanco	tobacconist's
el	euro	euro
los	grandes almacenes	department store
el	hipermercado	hypermarket
el	mercado	market
el	número (de zapato)	(shoe) size
el	precio	price
el	regalo	present
el	souvenir (pl ~s)	souvenir
el	supermercado	supermarket
el	talonario de cheques	cheque book
el	vendedor	salesman

USEFUL PHRASES

comprar/vender to buy/sell
¿cuánto cuesta? how much does it cost?
¿cuánto es? how much does it come to?
pagué veinte euros por esto, esto me costó veinte euros I paid 20 euros for that
en la carnicería/la panadería at the butcher's/bakery

ESSENTIAL WORDS (feminine)

la	agencia de viajes	travel agent's
la	alimentación	food
la	caja	checkout; cash desk
la	carnicería	butcher's
la	charcutería	pork butcher's
la	clienta	customer
la	compra	purchase
la	dependienta	shop assistant, sales assistant
la	farmacia	chemist's
la	floristería	flower shop
la	frutería	fruiterer's
la	lista	list
la	oficina de correos	post office
la	panadería	bakery
la	pastelería	cake shop
la	perfumería	perfume shop/department
la	pescadería	fishmonger's
la	rebaja	reduction
las	rebajas	sales
la	sección (pl secciones)	department
la	talla	size
la	tarjeta de crédito	credit card
la	tarjeta de débito	debit card
la	tienda	shop
la	tienda de alimentación or de comestibles	grocer's
la	vendedora	saleswoman
la	verdulería	greengrocer's
la	zapatería	shoe shop

IMPORTANT WORDS *(masculine)*

el	**artículo**	article
el	**carnicero**	butcher
el	**charcutero**	pork butcher
el	**comerciante**	shopkeeper
el	**comercio**	trade; shop
el	**comercio justo**	fair trade
el	**encargado**	manager
el	**frutero**	fruiterer
el	**mercadillo**	street market
el	**monedero**	purse
el	**mostrador**	counter
el	**panadero**	baker
el	**pastelero**	confectioner
el	**peluquero**	hairdresser
el	**pescadero**	fishmonger
el	**rastro** *(Sp)*	flea market
el	**recibo**	receipt
el	**tícket** *(pl ~s)*	receipt; ticket
el	**vendedor de periódicos**	newsagent
el	**verdulero**	greengrocer
el	**zapatero**	cobbler

USEFUL PHRASES

sólo estoy mirando I'm just looking
es demasiado caro it's too expensive
algo más barato something cheaper
es barato it's cheap
"pague en caja" "pay at the checkout"
¿lo quiere para regalo? would you like it gift-wrapped?
debe de haber un error there must be some mistake

IMPORTANT WORDS (feminine)

la **biblioteca**	library
la **boutique**	boutique
la **calculadora**	calculator
la **carnicera**	butcher
la **cartera**	wallet; purse; (LAm) handbag
la **charcutera**	pork butcher
la **comerciante**	shopkeeper
la **encargada**	manager
la **escalera mecánica**	escalator
la **frutera**	fruiterer
la **librería**	bookshop
la **marca**	brand
la **panadera**	baker
la **pastelera**	confectioner
la **peluquera**	hairdresser
la **pescadera**	fishmonger
la **promoción** (pl promociones)	special offer
la **reclamación** (pl reclamaciones)	complaint
la **tintorería**	dry-cleaner's
la **vendedora de periódicos**	newsagent
la **verdulera**	greengrocer
la **vitrina**	display case; (LAm) shop window

USEFUL PHRASES

¿**algo más?** anything else?
S.A. (= Sociedad Anónima) Ltd
S.L. (= Sociedad Limitada) limited liability company
y Cía & Co
"de venta aquí" "on sale here"
un coche de ocasión a used car
en oferta, de oferta on special offer
el café de comercio justo fair-trade coffee

USEFUL WORDS *(masculine)*

el	**agente inmobiliario**	estate agent
el	**color**	colour
el	**escaparate**	shop window
el	**ferretero**	ironmonger
el	**gerente**	manager
el	**joyero**	jeweller; jewellery box
el	**librero**	bookseller
el	**óptico**	optician
el	**producto**	product
los	**productos**	produce
el	**recado**	errand
el	**relojero**	watchmaker; clockmaker
el	**tendero**	grocer
el	**trato**	deal
el	**videoclub** *(pl ~s)*	video shop

USEFUL PHRASES

ir a ver escaparates, ir de escaparates to go window shopping
horario opening hours
pagar en metálico to pay cash
pagar con un cheque to pay by cheque
pagar con tarjeta de crédito to pay by credit card

USEFUL WORDS *(feminine)*

la	**agencia de viajes**	travel agent's
la	**agencia inmobiliaria**	estate agent's
la	**agente inmobiliario**	estate agent
la	**caja de ahorros**	savings bank
la	**cola**	queue
la	**compra**	purchase; shopping
las	**compras**	shopping
la	**confitería**	sweetshop
la	**droguería**	hardware shop
la	**ferretera**	ironmonger
la	**ferretería**	ironmonger's
la	**gerente**	manager
la	**joyera**	jeweller
la	**joyería**	jeweller's
la	**lavandería**	laundry
la	**librería**	bookseller
la	**mercancía**	goods
la	**óptica**	optician; optician's
la	**papelería**	stationer's
la	**rebaja**	discount
la	**relojera**	watchmaker; clockmaker
la	**relojería**	watchmaker's; clockmaker's
la	**sucursal**	branch
la	**talla de cuello**	collar size
la	**tendera**	grocer
la	**venta**	sale

USEFUL PHRASES

en el escaparate in the window
ir de compras to go shopping
hacer la compra to do the shopping
gastar to spend

ESSENTIAL WORDS (*masculine*)

el **aerobic**	aerobics
el **ajedrez**	chess
el **arco** (*LAm*)	goal
el **balón** (*pl* balones)	ball (*large*)
el **baloncesto**	basketball
el **balonvolea**	volleyball
el **billar**	billiards
el **campeón** (*pl* campeones)	champion
el **campeonato**	championship
el **campo**	field, (*football*) pitch; (*golf*) course; (*basketball*) court
el **ciclismo**	cycling
el **crícket**	cricket
el **deporte**	sport
el **equipo**	team
el **esquí**	skiing; ski
el **esquí acuático**	water skiing
el **estadio**	stadium
el **fútbol**	football
el **gimnasta**	gymnast
el **golf**	golf
el **hockey**	hockey
el **juego**	game; play
el **jugador**	player
el **partido**	match, game
el **paseo**	walk
el **resultado**	result
el **rugby**	rugby
el **tenis**	tennis

USEFUL PHRASES

jugar al fútbol/tenis to play football/tennis
marcar un gol/un punto to score a goal/a point
llevar la cuenta de los tantos to keep the score
el campeón/la campeona del mundo the world champion
ganar/perder un partido to win/lose a match
mi deporte preferido my favourite sport

ESSENTIAL WORDS *(feminine)*

la	**campeona**	champion
la	**cancha**	(*basketball/tennis*) court; (*LAm*) field, (*football*) pitch
la	**cancha de tenis** (*LAm*)	tennis court
la	**equitación**	horse-riding
la	**gimnasia**	gymnastics
la	**gimnasta**	gymnast
la	**jugadora**	player
la	**natación**	swimming
la	**partida**	game (*chess etc*)
la	**pelota**	ball
la	**pesca**	fishing
la	**piscina**	swimming pool
la	**pista**	track
la	**pista de tenis** (*Sp*)	tennis court
la	**portería**	goal
la	**tabla de windsurf**	windsurfing board
la	**vela**	sailing; sail

USEFUL PHRASES

empatar to equalize; to draw
correr to run; **saltar** to jump; **lanzar** to throw
ganar *or* **derrotar** *or* **vencer a algn** to beat sb
entrenarse to train
el Liverpool gana por 2 a 1 Liverpool is leading by 2 goals to 1
un partido de tenis a game of tennis
es socio de un club he belongs to a club
ir de pesca to go fishing
ir a la piscina to go to the swimming pool
¿sabes nadar? can you swim?
hacer deporte to do sport
montar en bicicleta *or* **hacer ciclismo** to go cycling
hacer vela to go sailing
hacer footing/alpinismo to go jogging/climbing
patín de cuchilla/de ruedas/en línea (ice) skate/roller skate/Rollerblade®
tiro al arco/al blanco archery/target practice

IMPORTANT WORDS *(masculine)*

los	**bolos**	skittles
el	**encuentro**	match

USEFUL WORDS *(masculine)*

el	**adversario**	opponent
el	**alpinismo**	mountaineering
el	**árbitro**	referee; umpire *(tennis)*
el	**atletismo**	athletics
el	**bádminton**	badminton
el	**boxeo**	boxing
el	**buceo**	diving
el	**chándal**	tracksuit
el	**cronómetro**	stopwatch
el	**descanso**	half-time
el	**entrenador**	trainer; coach
el	**espectador**	spectator
el	**footing**	jogging
el	**ganador**	winner
el	**gol**	goal
el	**hipódromo**	race course
los	**Juegos Olímpicos**	Olympic Games
el	**Mundial (de Fútbol)**	World Cup
el	**parapente**	paragliding
el	**patín**	skate
el	**patinaje sobre hielo**	(ice) skating
el	**perdedor**	loser
el	**portero**	goalkeeper
el	**principiante**	beginner
el	**remo**	rowing; oar
el	**resultado**	score
el	**salto de altura**	high jump
el	**salto de longitud**	long jump
el	**squash**	squash
el	**tanto**	goal; point
el	**tiro**	shooting
el	**torneo**	tournament
el	**trineo**	sledge

IMPORTANT WORDS *(feminine)*

la	**bola**	ball (*small*)
la	**carrera**	race
las	**carreras (de caballos)**	horse-racing
la	**defensa**	defence
la	**petanca**	pétanque
la	**pista de esquí**	ski slope

USEFUL WORDS *(feminine)*

la	**adversaria**	opponent
la	**árbitra**	referee; umpire (*tennis*)
la	**camiseta (de deporte)**	jersey, shirt
la	**caña de pescar**	fishing rod
la	**caza**	hunting
la	**copa**	cup
la	**Copa del Mundo**	World Cup
la	**eliminatoria**	heat
la	**entrenadora**	trainer, coach
la	**esgrima**	fencing
la	**espectadora**	spectator
la	**estación de esquí**	ski resort
	(*pl* estaciones de ~)	
la	**etapa**	stage
la	**final**	final
la	**ganadora**	winner
la	**jabalina**	javelin
la	**lucha libre**	wrestling
la	**perdedora**	loser
la	**pesca**	fishing
la	**pista de hielo**	ice rink
la	**pista de patinaje**	skating rink
la	**portera**	goalkeeper
la	**principiante**	beginner
la	**prórroga**	extra time
la	**raqueta**	racket
la	**red**	net
la	**tribuna**	stand
las	**zapatillas de deporte**	sports shoes; trainers
las	**zapatillas de tenis**	tennis shoes

ESSENTIAL WORDS *(masculine)*

el **actor**	actor
el **ambiente**	atmosphere
el **anfiteatro**	dress circle
el **asiento**	seat
el **auditorio**	auditorium; audience
el **boleto** *(LAm)*	ticket
el **cine**	cinema
el **circo**	circus
el **cómico**	comedian
el **espectáculo**	show
el **patio de butacas**	stalls
el **payaso**	clown
el **programa**	programme
el **público**	audience
el **teatro**	theatre
el **vestuario**	costume
el **videoclip** *(pl ~s)*	music video
el **western** *(pl ~s)*	western

IMPORTANT WORDS *(masculine)*

el **acomodador**	usher
el **actor principal**	leading man
el **ballet** *(pl ~s)*	ballet
el **cartel**	notice; poster
el **director**	director
el **entreacto**	interval
el **intermedio**	interval
el **maquillaje**	make-up

USEFUL PHRASES

ir al teatro/al cine to go to the theatre/to the cinema
reservar un asiento to book a seat
un asiento en el patio de butacas a seat in the stalls
mi actor preferido/actriz preferida my favourite actor/actress
durante el intermedio during the interval
salir a escena to come on stage
interpretar el papel de to play the part of

ESSENTIAL WORDS *(feminine)*

la **actriz** (*pl* actrices)	actress
la **banda sonora**	soundtrack
la **boletería** (*LAm*)	box office
la **cómica**	comedian
la **cortina**	curtain
la **entrada**	ticket
la **estrella de cine**	film star
la **música**	music
la **obra (de teatro)**	play
la **ópera**	opera
la **orquesta**	orchestra
la **payasa**	clown
la **película**	film
la **sala**	auditorium; cinema
la **salida**	exit
la **sesión** (*pl* sesiones)	performance; showing
la **taquilla**	box office

USEFUL PHRASES

interpretar to play
bailar to dance
cantar to sing
filmar una película to shoot a film
"próxima sesión: 21 horas" "next showing: 9 p.m."
"versión original" "original version"
"subtitulada" "subtitled"
"localidades agotadas" "full house"
aplaudir to clap
¡bis! encore!
¡bravo! bravo!
una película de ciencia ficción/de amor a science fiction film/a romance
una película de aventuras/de terror an adventure/horror film

IMPORTANT WORDS *(masculine continued)*

el	**primer actor**	leading man
el	**protagonista**	star
el	**subtítulo**	subtitle
el	**título**	title

USEFUL WORDS *(masculine)*

el	**anfiteatro**	circle
los	**aplausos**	applause
el	**apuntador**	prompter
el	**argumento**	plot
los	**bastidores**	wings
el	**crítico**	critic
el	**culebrón** (*pl* culebrones)	soap (opera)
el	**decorado**	scenery
el	**director de escena**	producer; stage manager
el	**dramaturgo**	playwright
el	**ensayo (general)**	(dress) rehearsal
el	**escenario**	stage; scene
el	**espectador**	member of the audience
el	**estrado**	platform
el	**estreno**	first night, premiere
el	**foco**	spotlight
el	**foso de la orquesta**	orchestra pit
el	**gallinero**	the "gods"
el	**guardarropa**	cloakroom
el	**guión** (*pl* guiones)	script
el	**guionista**	scriptwriter
el	**musical**	musical
el	**palco**	box
el	**papel**	part
el	**personaje**	character
el	**productor**	producer
el	**realizador**	director (*cinema*); producer (*TV*)
el	**regidor**	stage manager
el	**reparto**	cast
el	**serial**	serial
el	**vestíbulo**	foyer

IMPORTANT WORDS *(feminine)*

la	**acomodadora**	usherette
la	**actriz principal** *(pl* actrices ~es)	leading lady
la	**butaca**	seat
la	**cartelera**	hoarding, billboard;
		listings section
la	**comedia**	comedy
la	**directora**	director
la	**platea**	stalls
la	**primera actriz** *(pl* ~s actrices)	leading lady
la	**propina**	tip
la	**protagonista**	star
la	**reserva**	booking

USEFUL WORDS *(feminine)*

la	**actuación** *(pl* actuaciones)	acting, performance
la	**apuntadora**	prompter
las	**candilejas**	footlights
la	**crítica**	review; critics; critic
la	**directora de escena**	producer; stage manager
la	**dramaturga**	playwright
la	**escena**	scene
la	**escenografía**	scenery
la	**espectadora**	member of the audience
la	**farsa**	farce
la	**función** *(pl* funciones)	performance
la	**guionista**	scriptwriter
la	**pantalla**	screen
la	**platea**	stalls
la	**productora**	producer
la	**puesta en escena**	production
la	**realizadora**	director *(cinema)*; producer *(TV)*
la	**regidora**	stage manager
la	**representación**	performance
	(pl representaciones)	
la	**serie**	series
la	**tragedia**	tragedy

ESSENTIAL WORDS *(masculine)*

el **año**	year
el **cuarto de hora**	quarter of an hour
el **despertador**	alarm clock
el **día**	day
el **fin de semana**	weekend
el **instante**	moment
el **mes**	month
el **minuto**	minute
el **momento**	moment
el **reloj**	watch; clock
el **segundo**	second
el **siglo**	century
el **tiempo**	time

USEFUL PHRASES

a mediodía at midday
a medianoche at midnight
pasado mañana the day after tomorrow
hoy today
hoy en día nowadays
anteayer, antes de ayer the day before yesterday
mañana tomorrow
ayer yesterday
hace dos días 2 days ago
dentro de dos días in 2 days
una semana a week
una quincena a fortnight
todos los días every day
¿a qué día estamos?, ¿qué día es hoy? what day is it?
¿cuál es la fecha de hoy? what's the date?
de momento at the moment
las tres menos cuarto a quarter to 3
las tres y cuarto a quarter past 3
en el siglo XXI in the 21st century
ayer por la noche last night, yesterday evening

ESSENTIAL WORDS *(feminine)*

la	**hora**	hour; time (*in general*)
la	**jornada**	day
la	**mañana**	morning
la	**media hora**	half an hour
la	**noche**	night; evening
la	**quincena**	fortnight
la	**semana**	week
la	**tarde**	afternoon; evening

USEFUL PHRASES

el año pasado/próximo last/next year
la semana/el año que viene next week/year
dentro de media hora in half an hour
una vez once
dos/tres veces two/three times
varias veces several times
tres veces al año three times a year
nueve de cada diez veces nine times out of ten
érase una vez once upon a time there was
diez a la vez ten at a time
¿qué hora es? what time is it?
¿tiene hora? have you got the time?
son las seis/las seis menos diez/las seis y media it is 6 o'clock/10 to 6/
    half past 6
son las dos en punto it is 2 o'clock exactly
hace un rato a while ago
dentro de un rato in a while
temprano early
tarde late
esta noche (*past*) last night; (*to come*) tonight

IMPORTANT WORDS *(masculine)*

el	**día siguiente**	next day
el	**futuro**	future; future tense
el	**pasado**	past; past tense
el	**presente**	present (*time*); present tense
el	**retraso**	delay

USEFUL WORDS *(masculine)*

el	**año bisiesto**	leap year
el	**calendario**	calendar
el	**cronómetro**	stopwatch
el	**reloj de pie**	grandfather clock
el	**reloj de pulsera**	wristwatch

USEFUL PHRASES

pasado mañana the day after tomorrow
dos días después two days later
el día antes *or* **el día anterior** the day before
un día sí y otro no every other day
en el futuro in the future
un día libre a day off
un día de fiesta a public holiday
un día laborable a weekday
en un día de lluvia, en un día lluvioso on a rainy day
al amanecer, al alba at dawn
la mañana/tarde siguiente the following morning/evening
ahora now

USEFUL WORDS *(feminine)*

las	**agujas**	hands (*of clock*)
la	**década**	decade
la	**Edad Media**	Middle Ages
la	**época**	time; era
la	**esfera**	face (*of clock*)
las	**manecillas**	hands (*of clock*)

USEFUL PHRASES

llegas tarde you are late
llegas temprano you are early
este reloj adelanta/atrasa this watch is fast/slow
llegar a tiempo, llegar a la hora to arrive on time
¿cuánto tiempo? how long?
el tercer milenio the third millennium
no levantarse hasta tarde to have a lie-in
de un momento a otro any minute now
dentro de una semana in a week's time
el lunes que viene no el otro a week on Monday
la noche antes, la noche anterior the night before
en esa época at that time

ESSENTIAL WORDS *(masculine)*

el	**bricolaje**	DIY
el	**manitas** *(pl inv)*	handyman
el	**taller**	workshop

USEFUL WORDS *(masculine)*

el	**alambre (de espino)**	(barbed) wire
los	**alicates**	pliers
el	**andamio**	scaffolding
el	**candado**	padlock
el	**celo** *(Sp)*	Sellotape®
el	**chinche** *(LAm)*	drawing pin
el	**cincel**	chisel
el	**clavo**	nail
el	**destornillador**	screwdriver
el	**durex®** *(LAm)*	Sellotape®
el	**martillo**	hammer
el	**muelle**	spring
el	**pico**	pickaxe
el	**pincel**	paintbrush
el	**taladro**	drill
el	**tornillo**	screw

USEFUL PHRASES
hacer bricolaje, hacer chapuzas to do odd jobs
clavar un clavo con el martillo to hammer in a nail
"recién pintado(a)" "wet paint"
pintar to paint
empapelar to wallpaper

ESSENTIAL WORDS (feminine)

la	cuerda	rope
la	herramienta	tool
la	llave	key; (LAm) tap
la	llave inglesa	spanner
la	manitas (pl inv)	handywoman
la	máquina	machine

USEFUL WORDS (feminine)

la	aguja	needle
la	batería	battery (in car)
la	caja de herramientas	toolbox
la	cerradura	lock
la	chinche (LAm)	drawing pin
la	chincheta (Sp)	drawing pin
la	cola	glue
la	escalera (de mano)	ladder
la	goma (elástica)	rubber band
la	horca	(garden) fork
la	lima	file
la	obra	construction site
la	pala	spade
la	pila	battery (in radio etc)
la	sierra	saw
la	tabla	plank
la	taladradora	pneumatic drill
las	tijeras	scissors

USEFUL PHRASES

"prohibido el paso a la obra" "construction site: keep out"
práctico(a) handy
cortar to cut
reparar to mend
atornillar to screw (in)
desatornillar to unscrew

ESSENTIAL WORDS *(masculine)*

los	**alrededores**	surroundings
el	**aparcamiento** *(Sp)*	car park; parking space
el	**autobús** *(pl autobuses)*	bus
el	**ayuntamiento**	town hall; town council
el	**banco**	bank; bench
el	**barrio**	district
el	**bloque de departamentos** *(LAm)*	block of flats
el	**bloque de pisos** *(Sp)*	block of flats
el	**café**	café; coffee
el	**carro** *(LAm)*	car
el	**centro de la ciudad**	town centre
el	**cine**	cinema
el	**coche** *(Sp)*	car
el	**edificio**	building
el	**estacionamiento** *(LAm)*	car park; parking space
el	**habitante**	inhabitant
el	**hotel**	hotel
el	**mercado**	market
el	**metro**	underground, subway
el	**museo**	museum; art gallery
el	**parking** *(pl ~s)*	car park
el	**parque**	park
el	**peatón** *(pl peatones)*	pedestrian
el	**policía**	policeman
el	**puente**	bridge
el	**restaurante**	restaurant
el	**suburbio**	suburb; slum area
el	**taxi**	taxi
el	**teatro**	theatre
el	**tour** *(pl ~s)*	tour
el	**turista**	tourist

ESSENTIAL WORDS *(feminine)*

la **boutique**	boutique
la **calle**	street
la **carretera**	road
la **catedral**	cathedral
la **ciudad**	town, city
la **comisaría**	police station
la **contaminación**	air pollution
la **esquina**	corner
la **estación (de trenes)** (*pl* estaciones (~~))	(train) station
la **estación de autobuses** (*pl* estaciones ~~)	bus station
la **fábrica**	factory
la **gasolinera**	petrol station
la **habitante**	inhabitant
la **lavandería automática**	launderette
la **oficina**	office
la **oficina de correos**	post office
la **parada de autobús**	bus stop
la **parada de taxis**	taxi rank
la **piscina**	swimming pool
la **plaza**	square
la **policía**	policewoman; police
la **tienda**	shop
la **torre**	tower
la **turista**	tourist
la **vista**	view
la **vivienda de protección oficial**	council flat

USEFUL PHRASES

voy a la ciudad *or* **al centro** I'm going into town
en el centro (de la ciudad) in the town centre
en la plaza in the square
una calle de sentido único a one-way street
una zona muy urbanizada a built-up area
"dirección prohibida" "no entry"
cruzar la calle to cross the road

IMPORTANT WORDS *(masculine)*

el	**abono**	season ticket
el	**agente (de policía)**	police officer
el	**alcalde**	mayor
el	**atasco**	traffic jam
el	**cartel**	notice; poster
el	**castillo**	castle
el	**cibercafé**	internet café
el	**cruce**	crossroads
los	**jardines públicos**	park
el	**lugar**	place
el	**monumento**	monument
el	**parquímetro**	parking meter
el	**quiosco de periódicos**	news stand
el	**semáforo**	traffic lights
el	**sitio**	place
el	**tráfico**	traffic
el	**transeúnte**	passer-by
el	**zoológico**	zoo

USEFUL PHRASES

en la esquina de la calle at the corner of the street
vivir en las afueras to live in the outskirts
andar, caminar to walk
tomar el autobús/el metro, coger el autobús/el metro (*Sp*) to take the bus/the underground
comprar una tarjeta multiviajes to buy a multiple-journey ticket
picar to punch (*ticket*)

IMPORTANT WORDS *(feminine)*

la	**acera**	pavement
la	**agente (de policía)**	police officer
la	**alcaldesa**	mayor
la	**biblioteca**	library
la	**calle principal**	main street
la	**calzada**	road
la	**circulación**	traffic
la	**desviación** (*pl* desviaciones)	diversion
la	**estación de servicio** (*pl* estaciones ~ ~)	petrol station
la	**iglesia**	church
la	**máquina expendedora de billetes** (*Sp*) *or* **de boletos** (*LAm*)	ticket machine
la	**mezquita**	mosque
la	**parte antigua**	old town
la	**polución**	air pollution
la	**sinagoga**	synagogue
la	**tarjeta multiviajes**	multiple-journey ticket
la	**transeúnte**	passer-by
la	**zona azul**	restricted parking zone
la	**zona industrial**	industrial estate
la	**zona peatonal**	pedestrian precinct

USEFUL PHRASES

industrial industrial
histórico(a) historic
bonito(a) pretty
feo(a) ugly
limpio(a) clean
sucio(a) dirty

USEFUL WORDS *(masculine)*

el	**adoquín** *(pl* adoquines)	cobblestone
el	**barrio residencial**	residential area
el	**callejón sin salida** *(pl* callejones ~~)	cul-de-sac, dead end
el	**camino de bicicletas**	cycle path
el	**carril bici**	cycle lane
el	**cementerio**	cemetery
el	**ciudadano**	citizen
el	**cochecito (de niño)**	pram, buggy
el	**concejo municipal**	town council
el	**desfile**	parade
el	**distrito**	district
el	**edificio**	building
el	**embotellamiento**	traffic jam
el	**folleto**	leaflet
los	**lugares de interés**	sights, places of interest
el	**paradero de autobús** *(LAm)*	bus stop
el	**parque de bomberos** *(Sp)*	fire station
el	**paso de cebra**	zebra crossing
el	**paso de peatones**	pedestrian crossing
el	**pavimento**	road surface
el	**rascacielos** *(pl inv)*	skyscraper
el	**sondeo de opinión**	opinion poll

USEFUL WORDS *(feminine)*

las	**afueras**	outskirts
la	**alcantarilla**	sewer
la	**cafetería**	coffee shop, café; canteen
la	**calle sin salida**	cul-de-sac, dead end
la	**camioneta de reparto**	delivery van
la	**cárcel**	prison
la	**ciudadana**	citizen
la	**cola**	queue
la	**ciudad universitaria**	university campus
la	**curva**	bend
la	**estación de bomberos**	fire station
	(pl estaciones ~ ~) *(LAm)*	
la	**estatua**	statue
la	**farola**	street lamp
la	**flecha**	arrow
la	**galería de arte**	art gallery
la	**isla peatonal**	traffic island
la	**muchedumbre**	crowd
la	**multitud**	crowd
la	**muralla**	rampart
la	**parada de autobús**	bus stop
la	**población** *(pl* poblaciones)	population
la	**señal de tráfico**	road sign

ESSENTIAL WORDS *(masculine)*

el **andén** *(pl andenes)*	platform
el **asiento**	seat
el **AVE**	high-speed train
el **billete** *(Sp)*	ticket
el **billete de ida** *(Sp)*	single ticket
el **billete de ida y vuelta** *(Sp)*	return ticket
el **billete sencillo** *(Sp)*	single ticket
el **boleto** *(LAm)*	ticket
el **boleto de ida** *(LAm)*	single ticket
el **boleto de ida y vuelta** *(LAm)*	return ticket
el **bolso** *(Sp)*	handbag
el **compartimento**	compartment
el **descuento**	reduction
el **enlace**	connection
el **equipaje**	luggage
el **expreso**	fast train
el **freno**	brake
el **horario**	timetable
el **maletero**	porter
el **metro**	underground, subway
el **número**	number
el **oficial de aduanas**	customs officer
el **pasaporte**	passport
el **plano**	map
el **precio del billete** *(Sp)* or **del boleto** *(LAm)*	fare
el **puente**	bridge
el **recargo**	extra charge
el **retraso**	delay
el **taxi**	taxi
el **tícket** *(pl ~s)*	ticket; receipt
el **tren**	train
el **vagón** *(pl vagones)*	carriage
el **viaje**	journey
el **viajero**	traveller

ESSENTIAL WORDS *(feminine)*

la	**aduana**	customs
la	**bici**	bike
la	**bicicleta**	bicycle
la	**boletería** *(LAm)*	ticket office
la	**bolsa**	bag
la	**cafetería (de la estación)**	station buffet
la	**cantina (de la estación)**	station buffet
la	**cartera**	wallet; *(LAm)* handbag
la	**clase**	class
la	**conexión** *(pl* conexiones)	connection
la	**consigna**	left-luggage office
la	**consigna automática**	left-luggage locker
la	**dirección** *(pl* direcciones)	direction
la	**entrada**	entrance
la	**estación** *(pl* estaciones)	station
la	**estación de metro** *(pl* estaciones ~ ~)	underground station
la	**información**	information
la	**línea**	line
la	**llegada**	arrival
la	**maleta**	suitcase
la	**oficial de aduanas**	customs officer
la	**oficina de objetos perdidos**	lost property office
la	**parada de taxis**	taxi rank
la	**petaca** *(Mex)*	suitcase
la	**reserva**	reservation
la	**sala de espera**	waiting room
la	**salida**	departure; exit
la	**taquilla**	ticket office; locker
la	**vía**	track, line
la	**viajera**	traveller

USEFUL PHRASES

reservar un asiento to book a seat

pagar un recargo, pagar un suplemento to pay an extra charge, to pay
 a surcharge

hacer/deshacer el equipaje to pack/unpack

IMPORTANT WORDS *(masculine)*

el **coche-cama** *(pl ~s~)*	sleeping car
el **coche-comedor** *(pl ~s~)*	dining car
el **conductor**	driver
el **destino**	destination
el **ferrocarril**	railway
el **revisor**	ticket collector

USEFUL WORDS *(masculine)*

el **abono**	season ticket
el **baúl**	trunk
el **carnet joven** *(pl ~s ~)*	young persons' discount card
el **coche**	carriage
el **descarrilamiento**	derailment
el **jefe de estación**	stationmaster
el **maquinista**	engine-driver
el **panel informativo**	noticeboard
el **paso a nivel**	level crossing
el **silbato**	whistle
el **suplemento**	extra charge, supplement
el **trayecto**	journey
el **(tren de) mercancías** *(pl (~es ~) ~)*	goods train

USEFUL PHRASES

tomar el tren, coger el tren *(Sp)* to take the train
perder el tren to miss the train
montarse en el tren to get on the train
bajar del tren to get off the train
¿está libre este asiento? is this seat free?
el tren lleva retraso the train is late
un vagón de fumadores/no fumadores a smoking/ non-smoking
  compartment
"prohibido asomarse por la ventanilla" "do not lean out of the window"

IMPORTANT WORDS *(feminine)*

la	**barrera**	barrier
la	**conductora**	driver
la	**duración** (*pl* duraciones)	length (of time)
la	**escalera mecánica**	escalator
la	**frontera**	border
la	**litera**	couchette
la	**propina**	tip
la	**RENFE**	Spanish Railway
la	**revisora**	ticket collector
la	**tarifa**	fare

USEFUL WORDS *(feminine)*

la	**alarma**	alarm
la	**etiqueta**	label
la	**jefa de estación**	stationmaster
la	**locomotora**	locomotive
la	**maquinista**	engine-driver
la	**vía férrea**	(railway) line or track
las	**vías**	rails

USEFUL PHRASES

te acompañaré a la estación I'll go to the station with you
iré a buscarte a la estación I'll come and pick you up at the station
el tren de las diez con destino a/procedente de Madrid the 10 o'clock
   train to/from Madrid

ESSENTIAL WORDS (*masculine*)

el	**árbol**	tree
el	**bosque**	wood

USEFUL WORDS (*masculine*)

el	**abedul**	birch
el	**abeto**	fir tree
el	**acebo**	holly
el	**albaricoque**	apricot tree
el	**árbol frutal**	fruit tree
el	**arbusto**	bush
el	**arce**	maple
el	**boj**	box tree
el	**brote**	bud
el	**castaño**	chestnut tree
el	**cerezo**	cherry tree
el	**chabacano** (*Mex*)	apricot tree
el	**chopo**	poplar
el	**duraznero** (*LAm*)	peach tree
el	**espino**	hawthorn
el	**follaje**	foliage
el	**fresno**	ash
el	**huerto**	orchard
el	**limonero**	lemon tree
el	**manzano**	apple tree
el	**melocotonero** (*Sp*)	peach tree
el	**naranjo**	orange tree
el	**nogal**	walnut tree
el	**olmo**	elm
el	**peral**	pear tree
el	**pino**	pine
el	**platanero**	banana tree
el	**plátano**	plane tree
el	**roble**	oak
el	**sauce llorón** (*pl* ~s llorones)	weeping willow
el	**tejo**	yew
el	**tilo**	lime tree
el	**tronco**	trunk
el	**viñedo**	vineyard

ESSENTIAL WORDS *(feminine)*

la	**hoja**	leaf
la	**rama**	branch
la	**selva (tropical)**	rain forest

USEFUL WORDS *(feminine)*

la	**baya**	berry
la	**corteza**	bark
la	**encina**	ilex, holm oak
el	**haya** *(pl f* las hayas)	beech
la	**higuera**	fig tree
la	**raíz** *(pl* raíces)	root
la	**viña**	vineyard

ESSENTIAL WORDS *(masculine)*

el	**ajo**	garlic
los	**champiñones**	mushrooms
los	**chícharos** *(Mex)*	peas
los	**ejotes** *(Mex)*	French beans
los	**guisantes** *(Sp)*	peas
el	**pimiento**	pepper
el	**tomate**	tomato

USEFUL WORDS *(masculine)*

el	**apio**	celery
el	**berro**	watercress
el	**brécol**	broccoli
el	**calabacín** *(pl* calabacines*)*	courgette
el	**elote** *(Mex)*	sweetcorn
los	**espárragos**	asparagus
los	**frijoles** *(LAm)*	beans
los	**garbanzos**	chickpeas
el	**maíz (dulce** *or* **tierno)**	sweetcorn
el	**nabo**	turnip
el	**pepino**	cucumber
el	**perejil**	parsley
el	**pimiento morrón** *(pl ~s* morrones*)*	(sweet) pepper
el	**puerro**	leek
el	**rábano**	radish
el	**repollo**	cabbage

USEFUL PHRASES
cultivar verduras to grow vegetables
una mazorca de maíz *(Sp)*, **una mazorca de choclo** *(Mex)* corn on the cob

ESSENTIAL WORDS *(feminine)*

las	**arvejas** *(LAm)*	peas
la	**cebolla**	onion
la	**coliflor**	cauliflower
la	**ensalada**	salad
las	**habichuelas** *(LAm)*	French beans
las	**judías verdes** *(Sp)*	French beans
la	**papa** *(LAm, Southern Sp)*,	potato
la	**patata** *(Sp)*	
las	**verduras**	vegetables
la	**zanahoria**	carrot

USESFUL WORDS *(feminine)*

la	**alcachofa**	artichoke
las	**alubias** *(Sp)*	beans
la	**berenjena**	aubergine
la	**calabacita** *(Mex)*	courgette
la	**calabaza**	pumpkin
la	**cebolleta**	spring onion
la	**col**	cabbage
las	**coles de Bruselas**	Brussels sprouts
la	**endibia**	endive, chicory
la	**escarola**	curly endive
las	**espinacas**	spinach
las	**judías**	beans
las	**judías blancas**	haricot beans
la	**lechuga**	lettuce
las	**legumbres**	pulses
las	**lentejas**	lentils
la	**remolacha**	beetroot

USEFUL PHRASES

zanahoria rallada grated carrot
biológico(a) organic
vegetariano(a) vegetarian

ESSENTIAL WORDS (*masculine*)

el	**autobús** (*pl* autobuses)	bus
el	**autocar**	coach
el	**avión** (*pl* aviones)	plane
el	**barco de vela**	sailing ship; sailing boat
el	**bote**	boat
el	**bote de remos**	rowing boat
el	**camión** (*pl* camiones)	lorry
el	**carro**	cart; (*LAm*) car
el	**casco**	helmet
el	**ciclomotor**	moped
el	**coche** (*Sp*)	car
el	**coche de línea**	coach
el	**helicóptero**	helicopter
el	**medio de transporte**	means of transport
el	**metro**	underground, subway
el	**precio del billete** (*Sp*) *or* **del boleto** (*LAm*)	fare
el	**taxi**	taxi
el	**transbordador**	ferry
el	**transporte público**	public transport
el	**tren**	train
el	**vehículo**	vehicle
el	**vehículo pesado**	heavy goods vehicle

IMPORTANT WORDS (*masculine*)

el	**coche de bomberos**	fire engine

USEFUL PHRASES

viajar to travel
ha ido a Barcelona en avión he flew to Barcelona
tomar el autobús/el metro/el tren, coger (*Sp*) **el autobús/el metro/el tren**
  to take the bus/the subway/the train
montar en bicicleta to go cycling
se puede ir en coche you can go there by car

ESSENTIAL WORDS (feminine)

la **bici**	bike
la **bicicleta**	bicycle
la **camioneta**	van
la **caravana**	caravan
la **distancia**	distance
la **moto**	motorbike
la **motocicleta**	motorcycle, motorbike
la **parte de atrás**	back
la **parte de delante**	front
la **parte delantera**	front
la **parte trasera**	back
la **vespa®**	scooter

IMPORTANT WORDS (feminine)

la **ambulancia**	ambulance
la **grúa**	breakdown van

USEFUL PHRASES

reparar el coche de algn to repair sb's car
un coche de alquiler a hire car
un coche deportivo a sports car
un coche de carreras a racing car
un coche de empresa a company car
"coches de ocasión" "used cars"
arrancar to start, to move off

USEFUL WORDS (*masculine*)

el **aerodeslizador**	hovercraft
el **(barco de) vapor**	steamer
el **bulldozer** (*pl* ~s)	bulldozer
el **buque**	ship
el **camión articulado** (*pl* camiones ~s)	articulated lorry
el **camión cisterna** (*pl* camiones ~)	tanker
el **cochecito (de niño)**	pram, buggy
el **cohete**	rocket
el **hidroavión** (*pl* hidroaviones)	seaplane
el **jeep** (*pl* ~s)	jeep
el **navío**	ship
el **ovni (objeto volante no identificado)**	UFO (*unidentified flying object*)
el **petrolero**	oil tanker (*ship*)
el **planeador**	glider
el **platillo volante**	flying saucer
el **portaaviones** (*pl inv*)	aircraft carrier
el **remolcador**	tug
el **remolque**	trailer
el **riesgo**	risk
el **submarino**	submarine
el **tanque**	tank
el **teleférico**	cable car
el **telesilla**	chairlift
el **tranvía**	tram
el **velero**	sailing ship; sailing boat
el **velomotor**	moped
el **yate**	yacht; pleasure cruiser

USEFUL WORDS *(feminine)*

la	**barcaza**	barge
la	**camioneta de reparto**	delivery van
la	**canoa**	canoe
la	**carreta**	waggon; cart
la	**golondrina**	pleasure boat
la	**lancha**	boat (*small*); launch
la	**lancha de salvamento**	lifeboat
la	**lancha de socorro**	lifeboat
la	**lancha neumática**	rubber dinghy
la	**lancha rápida**	speedboat
la	**locomotora**	locomotive
la	**ranchera**	estate car

ESSENTIAL WORDS (*masculine*)

el	**aire**	air
el	**boletín meteorológico** (*pl* boletines ~s)	weather report
el	**calor**	heat
el	**cielo**	sky
el	**clima**	climate
el	**este**	east
el	**frío**	cold
el	**grado**	degree
el	**hielo**	ice
el	**invierno**	winter
el	**norte**	north
el	**oeste**	west
el	**otoño**	autumn
el	**paraguas** (*pl inv*)	umbrella
el	**parte meteorológico**	weather report
el	**pronóstico del tiempo**	(weather) forecast
el	**sol**	sun; sunshine
el	**sur**	south
el	**tiempo**	weather
el	**verano**	summer
el	**viento**	wind

USEFUL PHRASES

¿qué tiempo hace? what's the weather like?
hace calor/frío it's hot/cold
hace un día estupendo, hace un día precioso it's a lovely day
hace un día horrible it's a horrible day
al aire libre in the open air
hay niebla it's foggy
30° a la sombra 30° in the shade
escuchar el pronóstico del tiempo to listen to the weather forecast
llover to rain
nevar to snow
llueve it's raining
nieva it's snowing

ESSENTIAL WORDS *(feminine)*

la **estación** *(pl* estaciones)	season
la **lluvia**	rain
la **niebla**	fog
la **nieve**	snow
la **nube**	cloud
la **primavera**	spring
la **región** *(pl* regiones)	region, area
la **temperatura**	temperature

USEFUL PHRASES

brilla el sol the sun is shining
sopla el viento the wind is blowing
hace un frío que pela it's freezing
helarse to freeze
ha helado there's been a frost
fundirse to melt
soleado(a) sunny
tormentoso(a) stormy
lluvioso(a) rainy
frío(a) cool
variable changeable
húmedo(a) humid
el cielo está cubierto the sky is overcast

IMPORTANT WORDS (*masculine*)

el	**chaparrón** (*pl* chaparrones)	shower
el	**claro**	sunny spell
el	**humo**	smoke
el	**polvo**	dust

USEFUL WORDS (*masculine*)

el	**aguacero**	downpour
el	**amanecer**	dawn, daybreak
el	**anochecer**	nightfall, dusk
el	**arco iris** (*pl inv*)	rainbow
el	**barómetro**	barometer
el	**cambio**	change
el	**carámbano**	icicle
el	**charco**	puddle
el	**copo de nieve**	snowflake
el	**crepúsculo**	twilight
el	**deshielo**	thaw
el	**granizo**	hail
el	**huracán** (*pl* huracanes)	hurricane
el	**pararrayos** (*pl inv*)	lightning conductor
el	**quitanieves** (*pl inv*)	snowplough
el	**rayo**	lightning
el	**rayo de sol**	ray of sunshine
el	**relámpago**	flash of lightning
el	**rocío**	dew
el	**trueno**	thunder

IMPORTANT WORDS (*feminine*)

las **precipitaciones**	rainfall
la **previsión meteorológica** (*pl* previsiones ~s)	(weather) forecast
la **sombrilla**	parasol
la **tormenta**	storm
la **visibilidad**	visibility

USEFUL WORDS (*feminine*)

el **alba** (*pl f* las albas)	dawn
la **atmósfera**	atmosphere
la **brisa**	breeze
la **bruma**	mist
la **corriente (de aire)**	draught
la **escarcha**	frost (*on the ground*)
la **gota de lluvia**	raindrop
la **helada**	frost (*weather*)
la **inundación** (*pl* inundaciones)	flood
la **luz de la luna**	moonlight
la **mejora**	improvement
la **nevada**	snowfall
la **ola de calor**	heatwave
la **oscuridad**	darkness
la **puesta de sol**	sunset
la **ráfaga de viento**	gust of wind
la **sequía**	drought
la **tormenta**	thunderstorm
la **ventisca**	snowdrift

ESSENTIAL WORDS *(masculine)*

el	albergue juvenil	youth hostel
los	baños públicos *(LAm)*	toilets
el	bote de la basura *(Mex)*	dustbin
el	comedor	dining room
el	cuarto de baño	bathroom
el	cubo de la basura	dustbin
el	desayuno	breakfast
el	dormitorio	dormitory
los	lavabos	toilets
el	mapa	map
los	servicios *(Sp)*	toilets
el	silencio	silence
el	visitante	visitor

IMPORTANT WORDS *(masculine)*

el	carnet de socio *(pl ~s ~ ~)*	membership card
el	lavabo	washbasin; toilet
el	saco de dormir	sleeping bag

ESSENTIAL WORDS *(feminine)*

la	**cama**	bed
la	**(cama) litera**	bunk bed
la	**cocina**	kitchen; cooking
la	**comida**	meal
la	**ducha**	shower
la	**estancia**	stay
la	**lista de precios**	price list
la	**noche**	night
la	**oficina**	office
la	**sábana**	sheet
la	**sala de juegos**	games room
la	**tarifa**	rate(s)
las	**vacaciones**	holidays
la	**visitante**	visitor

IMPORTANT WORDS *(feminine)*

la	**caminata**	hike
la	**excursión** *(pl* excursiones)	trip
la	**guía**	guidebook
la	**mochila**	rucksack
las	**normas**	rules
la	**ropa de cama**	bed linen

USEFUL PHRASES

pasar una noche en el albergue juvenil to spend a night at the youth hostel

quisiera alquilar un saco de dormir I would like to hire a sleeping bag

está todo ocupado there's no more room

The vocabulary items on pages 204 to 233 have been grouped under parts of speech rather than topics because they can apply in a wide range of circumstances. Use them just as freely as the vocabulary already given.

ARTICLES AND PRONOUNS

What is an article?
In English, an **article** is one of the words *the*, *a* and *an* which is given in front of a noun.

What is a pronoun?
A **pronoun** is a word you use instead of a noun, when you do not need or want to name someone or something directly, for example, *it*, *you*, *none*.

algo something; anything
alguien somebody, someone; anybody, anyone
alguno/alguna one; someone, somebody
algunos/algunas some, some of them; some of us, some of you, some of them
ambos/ambas both
aquel/aquella; aquél/aquélla that
aquellos/aquellas; aquéllos/aquéllas those
cada each; every
cual which; who; whom
  lo cual which
cuál what, which one
cualquiera any one; anybody, anyone
  cualquiera de los dos/las dos either (*see also* Adjectives)
cualesquiera (*pl*) any (*see also* Adjectives)
cuanto/cuanta as much as
cuánto/cuánta how much
cuantos/cuantas as many as
cuántos/cuántas how many
cuyo/cuya/cuyos/cuyas whose

en cuyo caso in which case
demasiado/demasiada too much
demasiados too many
dos: los/las dos both
el/la the
él he; him; it
  de él his
ella she; her; it
  de ella hers
ello it
ellos/ellas they; them
  de ellos/ellas theirs
ese/esa; ése/ésa that
esos/esas; ésos/ésas those
este/esta; éste/ésta this
estos/estas; éstos/éstas these
la her; it; you
las them; you
le him; her; it; you
les them; you
lo him; it; you
los/las the
los them; you
me me; myself
mi/mis my
(el)mío/(la) mía/(los) míos/(las) mías mine

mismo/misma/mismos/mismas same
  mí mismo/misma; yo mismo/ misma myself; **nosotros mismos/ nosotras mismas** ourselves; **sí misma; ella misma** herself; **sí mismo; él mismo** himself; **sí mismos/sí mismas; ellos mismos/ellas mismas** themselves; **ti mismo/ti misma; tú mismo/ tú misma; usted mismo/usted misma** yourself; **vosotros mismos/vosotras mismas; ustedes mismos/ustedes mismas** yourselves; **uno mismo/una misma** oneself
mucho/mucha a lot, lots; much (see also Adjectives; Adverbs)
muchos/muchas a lot, lots; many (see also Adjectives)
nada nothing
  nada más nothing else
nadie nobody, no one; anybody, anyone
  nadie más nobody else
ninguno/ninguna any; neither; either; none; no one, nobody
  ninguno de los dos/ninguna de las dos neither (see also Adjectives)
ningunos/ningunas any; none (see also Adjectives)
nos us; ourselves; each other
nosotros/nosotras we; us
nuestro/nuestra/nuestros/ nuestras our; ours
  el nuestro/la nuestra/ los nuestros/las nuestras ours
os you; yourselves; each other
otro/otra another, another one (see also Adjectives)

otros/otras others (see also Adjectives)
poco/poca un poco a bit, a little
  dentro de poco shortly
pocos/pocas not many, few
que who; that
qué what; what a
quien/quienes who; whoever
quién/quiénes who
se him; her; them; you; himself; herself; itself; themselves; yourself; yourselves; oneself; each other
su/sus his; her; its; their; your; one's
(el) suyo/(la) suya /(los) suyos/ (las) suyas his; her; its; their; your; hers; theirs; yours; one's own
tal/tales such
tampoco not...either, neither
te you; yourself
ti you
todo/toda (it) all
  todo el mundo everybody, everyone (see also Adjectives)
todos/todas all; every; everybody; everyone (see also Adjectives)
tu/tus your
tú you
usted you
ustedes you
(el) tuyo/ (la) tuya/ (los) tuyos/(las) tuyas yours
un/una a; an; one
unos/unas some; a few; about, around
varios/varias several
vosotros/vosotras you
vuestro/vuestra/vuestros/ vuestras your; yours
  los vuestros/las vuestras yours
yo I; me

CONJUNCTIONS

> **What is a conjunction?**
> A **conjunction** is a word such as *and*, *but*, *or*, *so*, *if* and *because*, that links two words or phrases of a similar type, or two parts of a sentence, for example, *Diane <u>and</u> I have been friends for years*; *I left <u>because</u> I was bored*.

ahora though
  ahora bien however; **ahora que** now that
antes: antes de que before
así: así (es) que so
  así pues so
aunque although, though
como as
conque so, so then
consiguiente: por consiguiente so, therefore
cuando when; whenever; if
cuanto: en cuanto as soon as; as
dar: dado que since
decir: es decir that is to say
desde: desde que since
después: después de que after
e and
embargo: sin embargo still, however
entonces then
fin: a fin de que so that, in order that
forma: de forma que so that
hasta: hasta que until, till
luego therefore
manera: de manera que so that
mas but
más: más que more than
menos: menos que less than
mientras while; as long as
  mientras que whereas; **mientras**

(tanto) meanwhile
modo: de modo que so that
momento: en el momento en que just as
ni or; nor; even
  ni...ni neither...nor
o or
  o ... o ... either ... or ...
para: para que so that
pero but
porque because
pronto: tan pronto como as soon as
pues then; well; since
puesto: puesto que since
que that
ser: o sea that is
  a no ser que unless
si if; whether
  si no otherwise
siempre: siempre que whenever; as long as, provided that
sino but; except; only
tal: con tal (de) que as long as, provided that
tanto: por (lo) tanto so, therefore
u or
vez: una vez que once
vista: en vista de que seeing that
y and
ya: ya que as, since

ADJECTIVES

> **What is an adjective?**
> An **adjective** is a 'describing' word that tells you more about a person
> or thing, such as their appearance, colour, size or other qualities, for
> example, *pretty*, *blue*, *big*.

abierto(a) open
absoluto(a) absolute
absurdo(a) absurd
académico(a) academic
accesible accessible; approachable
aceptable acceptable
acondicionado(a) fitted out
  con aire acondicionado
  air-conditioned
acostumbrado(a) accustomed
activo(a) active
acusado(a) accused; marked
adecuado(a) appropriate
admirable admirable
aéreo(a) aerial
aficionado(a) keen
afilado(a) sharp
afortunado(a) fortunate, lucky
agitado(a) rough; agitated; hectic
agotado(a) exhausted
agradable pleasant, agreeable
agresivo(a) aggressive
agrícola agricultural
agudo(a) sharp; acute
aislado(a) isolated
alegre happy; bright; lively; merry
alguno/alguna (*before masc sing*
  algún) some; any (*see also* Articles
  and Pronouns)
algunos/algunas some; several
  (*see also* Articles and Pronouns)
alternativo(a) alternating; alternative

alto(a) high; tall
amargo(a) bitter
ancho(a) broad; wide
anciano(a) elderly
animado(a) lively; cheerful
anónimo(a) anonymous
anormal abnormal
anterior former
antiguo(a) old; vintage; antique
anual annual
apagado(a) out; off; muffled; dull
aparente apparent
apasionado(a) passionate
apropiado(a) appropriate, suitable
aproximado(a) rough
arriba: de arriba top
asequible affordable
asombrado(a) amazed, astonished
asombroso(a) amazing,
  astonishing
áspero(a) rough
atestado(a) crowded; popular
atento(a) attentive; watchful
atractivo(a) attractive
automático(a) automatic
avanzado(a) advanced
bajo(a) low; short
barba: con barba bearded
barbudo(a) bearded
básico(a) basic
bastante enough; quite a lot of
  (*see also* Adverbs)

bien well-to-do
bienvenido(a) welcome
blando(a) soft
breve brief
brillante shining; bright
brutal brutal
bruto(a) rough; stupid; uncouth; gross
bueno(a) good
cada each; every
caliente hot; warm
callado(a) quiet
cansado(a) tired
capaz capable
cariñoso(a) affectionate
caro(a) expensive, dear
cauteloso(a) cautious
central central
ceñido(a) tight
cercano(a) close; nearby
cerrado(a) closed; off
científico(a) scientific
cierto(a) true; certain
civil civil; civilian
claro(a) clear; light; bright
clásico(a) classical; classic
climatizado(a) air-conditioned
cobarde cowardly
comercial commercial
cómodo(a) comfortable
complejo(a) complex
completo(a) complete
complicado(a) complicated; complex
comprensivo(a) understanding
común common; mutual
concreto(a) specific; concrete
concurrido(a) crowded; popular
conmovedor(a) moving
consciente conscious; aware

conservador(a) conservative
considerable considerable
constante constant
contemporáneo(a) contemporary
contento(a) happy; pleased
continuo(a) continuous
convencional conventional
correcto(a) correct, right
corriente ordinary; common
cortado(a) cut; closed; off; shy
creativo(a) creative
cristiano(a) Christian
crítico(a) critical
crudo(a) raw
cuadrado(a) square
cualquiera (*before masc and fem sing*** cualquier)** any (*see also* Articles and Pronouns)
cualesquiera any (*see also* Articles and Pronouns)
cuanto/cuanta as much as
cuánto/cuánta how much
cuantos/cuantas as many as
cuántos/cuántas how many
cultural cultural
curioso(a) curious
debido(a) due, proper
decepcionante disappointing
decidido(a) determined
delicado(a) delicate
delicioso(a) delicious
demasiado/demasiada too much
demasiados too many
democrático(a) democratic
derecho(a) right
desafortunado(a) unfortunate
desagradable unpleasant
desconocido(a) unknown
desesperado(a) desperate

desierto(a) deserted
desnudo(a) naked; bare
despejado(a) clear
despierto(a) awake; sharp; alert
despreocupado(a) carefree; careless
destruido(a) destroyed
detallado(a) detailed
diestro(a) skilful
difícil difficult
digno(a) worthy; dignified
diminuto(a) tiny
directo(a) direct
disgustado(a) upset
disponible available
dispuesto(a) arranged; willing
distinguido(a) distinguished
distinto(a) different; various
divertido(a) funny, amusing; fun; entertaining
dividido(a) divided
divino(a) divine
doble double
domesticado(a) tame
doméstico(a) domestic
dos: los/las dos both
dulce sweet
duro(a) hard
económico(a) economic; economical
efectivo(a) effective
eficaz effective; efficient
eficiente efficient
eléctrico(a) electric
electrónico(a) electronic
elemental elementary
emocionante exciting
emotivo(a) emotional; moving
encantador(a) charming; lovely
enmascarado(a) masked
enorme enormous, huge

enterado(a) knowledgeable; well-informed; aware
entero(a) whole
equivalente equivalent
equivocado(a) wrong
escandaloso(a) shocking
esencial essential
especial special
específico(a) specific
espectacular spectacular
espeso(a) thick
espiritual spiritual
estrecho(a) narrow
estricto(a) strict
estropeado(a) broken (off); off
estupendo(a) marvellous, great
estúpido(a) stupid
étnico(a) ethnic
evidente obvious, evident
exacto(a) exact; accurate
excelente excellent
excepcional outstanding
exclusivo(a) exclusive
exigente demanding, exacting
experto(a) experienced
éxito: de éxito successful
exitoso(a) successful
exquisito(a) delicious; exquisite
extra extra; top-quality
extranjero(a) foreign
extraño(a) strange; foreign
extraordinario(a) extraordinary; outstanding; special
extremo(a) extreme
fácil easy
falso(a) false
familiar family; familiar
famoso(a) famous
fatigoso(a) tiring

federal federal
feroz fierce
fijo(a) fixed; permanent
final final
financiero(a) financial
fino(a) fine; smooth; refined
firme firm; steady
físico(a) physical
flexible flexible
fluido(a) fluid; fluent
formal reliable; formal; official
frágil fragile; frail
frecuente frequent
fresco(a) fresh; cool; cheeky
fuerte strong; loud
futuro(a) future
general general
generoso(a) generous
genial brilliant; wonderful
gentil kind
genuino(a) genuine
global global
gordo(a) fat; big
grande (*before masc sing* **gran**) big; great
grandioso(a) grand; grandiose
habitual usual
herido(a) injured; wounded; hurt
hermoso(a) beautiful
histórico(a) historic; historical
holgado(a) loose
honrado(a) honest; respectable
horrible horrific; hideous; terrible
horroroso(a) dreadful; hideous; terrible
humano(a) human; humane
ideal ideal
idéntico(a) identical
igual equal

ilegal illegal
iluminado(a) illuminated, lit; enlightened
ilustrado(a) illustrated
imaginario(a) imaginary
impar odd
importante important
imposible impossible
imprescindible indispensable
impresionante impressive; moving; shocking
inaguantable unbearable
incapaz (de) incapable (of)
increíble incredible; unbelievable
inculto(a) uncultured
indefenso(a) defenceless
independiente independent
indiferente unconcerned
individual individual; single
industrial industrial
inesperado(a) unexpected
inevitable inevitable
infantil childlike; childish
inflable inflatable
injusto(a) unfair
inmediato(a) immediate
inmenso(a) immense
inmune immune
inquieto(a) anxious; restless
intacto(a) intact
intencionado(a) deliberate
intenso(a) intense; intensive
interior interior; inside; inner; domestic
interminable endless
internacional international
interno(a) internal
interrumpido(a) interrupted
inútil useless

invisible invisible
izquierdo(a) left
junto(a) together
justo(a) just, fair; exact; tight
largo(a) long
legal legal
lento(a) slow
libre free
ligero(a) light; slight; agile
limpio(a) clean
liso(a) smooth; straight; plain
listo(a) ready; bright
llamativo(a) bright; striking
llano(a) flat; straightforward
lleno(a) (de) full (of)
lluvioso(a) rainy, wet
loco(a) mad, crazy
lujo: de lujo luxurious
lujoso(a) luxurious
magnífico(a) magnificent;
  wonderful, superb
maligno(a) malignant; evil, malicious
malo(a) bad
malvado(a) wicked
manso(a) meek; tame
maravilloso(a) marvellous,
  wonderful; magic
marcado(a) marked
más more of a
máximo(a) maximum
mayor bigger; elder
  el/la...mayor the biggest...;
  the eldest...
mecánico(a) mechanical
médico(a) medical
medio(a) half; average
medioambiental environmental
mejor better
  el/la mejor the best

menor smaller; younger
  el/la...menor the smallest;
  the youngest
menos less of a
mental mental
militar military
minucioso(a) thorough; very
  detailed
mismo(a) same
misterioso(a) mysterious
moderado(a) moderate
moderno(a) modern
mojado(a) wet; soaked
molesto(a) annoying; annoyed;
  awkward; uncomfortable
montañoso(a) mountainous
mucho/mucha a lot of, lots of;
  much (*see also* Pronouns; Adverbs)
muchos/muchas a lot of, lots of;
  many (*see also* Pronouns)
muerto(a) dead
mundial worldwide, global
mutuo(a) mutual
nacido(a) born
nacional national; domestic
nativo(a) native
natural natural
necesario(a) necessary
negativo(a) negative
ninguno/ninguna (*before masc sing***
  ningún)** no; any (*see also*
  Pronouns)
ningunos/ningunas no; any
  (*see also* Pronouns)
normal normal; standard
nuclear nuclear
nuevo(a) new
numeroso(a) numerous
obediente obedient

objetivo(a) objective
obligatorio(a) compulsory, obligatory
obvio(a) obvious
ocupado(a) busy; taken; engaged; occupied
oficial official
oportuno(a) opportune; appropriate
original original
oscuro(a) dark; obscure
otro/otra another
  a/en otro lugar somewhere else; **otra cosa** something else; **otra persona** somebody else; **otra vez** again (*see also* Pronouns); **otros/ otras** other (*see also* Pronouns)
pacífico(a) peaceful; peaceable
pálido(a) pale
par even
particular special; particular; private
patético(a) pathetic
peligroso(a) dangerous
peor worse
  el peor the worst
perdido(a) lost; stray; remote
perfecto(a) perfect
personal personal
pesado(a) heavy; tedious
picante hot
pie: de pie standing (up)
poco/poca not much, little
pocos/pocas not many, few
poderoso(a) powerful
polémico(a) controversial
polvoriento(a) dusty; powdery
popular popular
portátil portable
posible possible; potential

positivo(a) positive
práctico(a) practical
precioso(a) lovely, beautiful; precious
preciso(a) precise; necessary
preferido(a) favourite
preliminar preliminary
presentable presentable
presunto(a) alleged
previo(a) previous
primario(a) primary
principal main
privado(a) private
privilegiado(a) privileged
profundo(a) deep
prometido(a) promised; engaged
propio(a) own
próximo(a) near, close; next
psicológico(a) psychological
público(a) public
pueril childish
pulcro(a) neat
puntiagudo(a) pointed; sharp
puntual punctual
puro(a) pure
qué what; which; what a
querido(a) dear
químico(a) chemical
racial racial
radical radical
rápido(a) fast, quick
raro(a) strange, odd; rare
razonable reasonable
reacio(a) reluctant
real actual; royal
reciente recent
recto(a) straight; honest
redondo(a) round
refrescante refreshing

regional regional
regular regular
religioso(a) religious
repentino(a) sudden
repuesto: de repuesto spare
reservado(a) reserved
resistente resistant; tough
responsable (de) responsible (for)
revolucionario(a) revolutionary
ridículo(a) ridiculous
rival rival
romántico(a) romantic
rubio(a) fair, blond
ruidoso(a) noisy
rural rural
sabio(a) wise
sagrado(a) sacred
salvaje wild
salvo: a salvo safe
sanitario(a) sanitary; health
sano(a) healthy
  sano(a) y salvo(a) safe and sound
santo(a) holy
satisfecho(a) (de) satisfied (with)
seco(a) dry
secreto(a) secret
secundario(a) secondary
seguro(a) safe; secure; certain; sure
semejante similar
sencillo(a) simple; natural; single
sensacional sensational
sentado(a) sitting, seated
señalado(a) special
separado(a) separate
servicial helpful
severo(a) severe
sexual sexual
significativo(a) significant;
  meaningful

siguiente next, following
silencioso(a) silent; quiet
sincero(a) sincere
singular singular; outstanding
siniestro(a) sinister
situado(a) situated
sobra: de sobra spare
sobrante spare
social social
solemne solemn
sólido(a) solid
 solo(a) alone; lonely; black;
  straight, neat
soltero(a) single
sombrío(a) sombre; dim
sonriente smiling
soportable bearable
sorprendente surprising
sospechoso(a) suspicious
suave smooth; gentle; mild; slight
sucio(a) dirty
superior top; upper; superior
supremo(a) supreme
supuesto(a) assumed; supposed
tal/tales such
tanto/tanta so much
tantos/tantas so many
técnico(a) technical
terrible terrible
típico(a) typical
tirante tight; tense
todo/toda all (*see also* Pronouns)
todos/todas all; every (*see also*
  Pronouns)
tolerante broad-minded
total total
tradicional traditional
tremendo(a) tremendous
triste sad

último(a) last
  el último the latest
ultrajante offensive; outrageous
único(a) only; unique
urgente urgent
útil useful, helpful
vacante vacant
vacío(a) empty
valiente brave, ourageous
valioso(a) valuable
valor: de valor valuable
variado(a) varied

varios/varias several
vecino(a) neighbouring
verdad: de verdad real
verdadero(a) real; true
viejo(a) old
vil villainous; vile
violento(a) violent; awkward
visible visible
vital vital
vivo(a) living; alive; lively
voluntario(a) voluntary

ADVERBS AND PREPOSITIONS

> **What is an adverb?**
> An **adverb** is a word usually used with verbs, adjectives or other adverbs that gives more Information about when, how, where, or in what circumstances something happens, or to what degree something is true, for example, *quickly*, *happily*, *now*, *extremely*, *very*.
>
> **What is a preposition?**
> A **preposition** is a word such as *at*, *for*, *with*, *into* or *from*, which is usually followed by a noun, pronoun, or, in English, a word ending in -ing. Prepositions show how people or things relate to the rest of the sentence, for example, *She's at home*; *a tool for cutting grass*; *It's from David*.

a to; at; into: onto
abajo down; downstairs; below
  allá abajo down there
absolutamente absolutely
acá here, over here; now
acerca: acerca de about
actualmente at present
acuerdo: de acuerdo OK, okay
adelante forward
  en adelante from now on
  hacia adelante forward
además also; furthermore, moreover, in addition
  además de as well as; besides
admirablemente admirably
afortunadamente fortunately
agradablemente nicely
ahora now; in a minute
  hasta ahora so far
alcance: al alcance within reach
allá there, over there
allí there
alrededor de around
ansiosamente anxiously
ante before; in the face of; faced with

ante todo above all
antemano: de antemano beforehand, in advance
anteriormente previously, before
antes before **antes de** before
  cuanto antes as soon as possible
  lo antes posible as soon as possible
apartado: apartado de away from
aparte: aparte de apart from
apenas hardly, scarcely; only
aproximadamente approximately
aquí here; now
arriba up; upstairs; above
  allá arriba up there
así like that; like this
  así como as well as
atentamente attentively, carefully; kindly
atrás behind; at the back; backwards; ago
  hacia atrás backwards
aun even **aun así** even so
  aun cuando even if
aún still, yet; even
azar: al azar at random

bajo low; quietly; under
básicamente basically
bastante enough; quite a lot; quite
(*see also* Adjectives)
bien well; carefully; very; easily
brevemente briefly
bruscamente abruptly
cambio: a cambio de in exchange
for; in return for
en cambio instead
camino: de camino on the way
casi almost, nearly
caso: en el caso de (que) in the case of
en todo caso in any case
casualidad: por casualidad by
chance
causa: a causa de because of
cerca (de) close (to); near (to)
claramente clearly
cómo how
como like; such as; as; about
completamente completely
con with
concreto: en concreto specifically,
in particular
continuamente constantly
contra against
correctamente correctly
cortésmente politely
cuando when
cuándo when
cuanto: en cuanto a as regards, as for
cuánto how much; how far; how
cuenta: a fin de cuentas ultimately
teniendo en cuenta considering
cuidado: con cuidado carefully
cuidadosamente carefully
curiosamente curiously
curso: en el curso de in the course of

de of; from; about; by; than; in; if
debajo underneath
debajo de under; **por debajo**
underneath; **por debajo de** under;
below
débilmente faintly; weakly
delante in front; at the front;
opposite
delante de in front of; opposite
hacia delante forward
por delante ahead; at the front
demasiado too; too much
dentro inside
dentro de inside; in; within
deprisa quickly, hurriedly
derecha: a la derecha on the right
desde from; since
desgraciadamente unfortunately
despacio slowly
después later; after(wards); then
después de after
detrás behind; at the back; on the
back; after
detrás de behind; **por detrás** from
behind; on the back
día: al día per day
diariamente on a daily basis
diario: a diario daily
donde where; wherever
dónde where
dondequiera anywhere
duda: sin duda definitely,
undoubtedly
dulcemente sweetly; gently
durante during; for
durante todo/toda throughout
efecto: en efecto in fact
ejemplo: por ejemplo for example
en in; on; at; into; by

encima on top
  encima de above; on top of; **por**
  encima over; **por encima de** over;
  above
enfrente (de) opposite
enseguida right away
entonces then
  desde entonces since then; **hasta**
  entonces until then
entre among(st); between
especialmente especially,
  particularly; specially
evidentemente obviously, evidently
exactamente exactly
excepción: con la excepción de
  with the exception of
excepto except (for)
extranjero: en el extranjero
  overseas; abroad
extremadamente extremely
fácilmente easily
fielmente faithfully
fin: por fin finally; at last
finalmente eventually
forma: de alguna forma somehow
  de esta forma like that; like this;
  de ninguna forma in no way;
  de otra forma otherwise;
  de todas formas anyway
francamente frankly; really
frecuentemente frequently
frente: frente a opposite, facing;
  against
fuera outside; out
  fuera de outside
gana: de buena gana willingly,
  happily
  de mala gana reluctantly
general: por lo general as a rule

generalmente generally
gracias: gracias a thanks to
gradualmente gradually
hacia towards
hasta to, as far as; up to; down to;
  until
honradamente honestly
igualmente equally; likewise
incluido including
inmediatamente immediately
intensamente intensely
izquierda: a la izquierda on the left
jamás never; ever
junto: junto a close to, near; next
  to; together with
  junto con together with
justamente just; exactly; justly
lado: al lado (de) next door (to); near
  al lado de alongside; **al otro lado de**
  across; **de un lado a otro** to and fro;
  por este lado (de) on this side (of)
largo: a lo largo de along
lejos (de) far (from)
ligeramente lightly; slightly
luego then; later, afterwards
  desde luego certainly
mal badly; poorly; ill
manera: de alguna manera
  somehow
  de esta manera like that; like this;
  de ninguna manera in no way; **de**
  otra manera otherwise; **de todas**
  maneras anyway
más more; plus
  el/la más the most; **más allá de**
  beyond; **más bien** rather; **más**
  cerca closer; **más lejos** further;
  más o menos about; **más...que**
  more...than; **no más** no more

medio: en medio de in the middle of
  por medio de by means of
mejor better
  el mejor the best
menos less; minus
  el/la menos the least;
  menos…que less than; **por lo
  menos** at least
mentalmente mentally
menudo: a menudo often
misteriosamente mysteriously
modo: de algún modo somehow
  de este modo like that; like this;
  de ningún modo in no way; **de
  otro modo** otherwise; **de todos
  modos** anyway
momento: en este momento at
  the moment
  en ese mismo momento at that
  very moment
mucho a lot
  no mucho not much (*see also*
  Pronouns; Adjectives)
muy very
naturalmente naturally
nerviosamente nervously
no no; not
nombre: en nombre de on behalf of
normalmente normally; usually
novedad: sin novedad safely
nunca never; ever
paciencia: con paciencia patiently
para for; to
  para atrás backwards; **para la
  derecha** towards the right; **para
  siempre** forever
parte: de mi parte on my behalf
  en cualquier parte anywhere;
  en gran parte largely

en otra parte elsewhere
  en parte partly, in part; **en todas
  partes** everywhere; **por otra
  parte** on the other hand
peligrosamente dangerously
peor worse
  el peor the worst
perfectamente perfectly
persona: por persona per person
personalmente personally
pesadamente heavily
pesar: a pesar de despite; in spite of
  a pesar de que even though
pie: a pie on foot
poco not very; not a lot; not much
  poco a poco little by little, bit by bit
por because of; for; by; through
  por qué why
precisamente precisely, exactly
primero first
principalmente mainly
principio: al principio at first
probable likely
probablemente probably
profundamente deeply
pronto soon
propósito: a propósito deliberately;
  on purpose
qué how
querer: sin querer accidentally
quién: de quién/de quiénes whose
rápidamente fast, quickly
rápido quickly
realidad: en realidad in fact, actually
realmente really
recientemente recently, lately
regularmente regularly, on a
  regular basis
relativamente relatively

repente: de repente suddenly
seguida: en seguida right away
seguido straight on
  todo seguido straight on
según according to; depending on
seguramente probably; surely
sencillamente simply
sentido: en este sentido in this
  respect
separado: por separado separately
ser: a no ser que unless
serio: en serio seriously
sí yes
siempre always
  como siempre as usual
siguiente: al/el día siguiente next
  day
silencio: en silencio quietly; in
  silence
silenciosamente quietly, silently
sin without **sin embargo** still,
  however, nonetheless
siquiera: ni siquiera not even
sitio: en algún sitio somewhere
  en ningún sitio nowhere
sobre on; over; about
solamente only; solely
sólo only; solely
  tan sólo only, just
suavemente gently; softly; smoothly
suelo: al suelo to the ground
  en el suelo on the ground
sumamente highly, extremely
supuesto: por supuesto of course
tal: tal como just as
  tal y como están las cosas under
  the circumstances; **tal vez**
  perhaps, maybe
también also, too

tampoco not...either, neither
tan so; such
  tan ... como as ... as
tanto so much; so often
  tanto más all the more
tarde late
  más tarde later; afterwards
temprano early
  más temprano earlier
tiempo: a tiempo in time; on time
  al mismo tiempo at the same
  time; **mucho tiempo** long
todavía still; yet; even
todo: en todo/toda throughout
  todo lo más at (the) most
total in short; at the end of the day
  en total altogether, in all
totalmente totally, completely
través: a través de through; across
vano: en vano in vain
velocidad: a toda velocidad at full
  speed, at top speed
ver: por lo visto apparently
vez: algunas veces sometimes
  cada vez más more and more;
  cada vez menos less and less; **de
  vez en cuando** from time to time,
  now and then; **en vez de** instead
  of; **rara vez** rarely, seldom; **una
  vez** once; **una vez más** once more
vía: en vías de on its way to
  en vías de desarrollo developing;
  en vías de extinción endangered
vista: de vista by sight
  en vista de in view of
voz: en voz alta aloud; loudly
  en voz baja in a low voice
ya already
  ya mismo at once; **ya no** not any
  more, no longer

SOME EXTRA NOUNS

> **What is a noun?**
> A **noun** is a 'naming' word for a living being, thing or idea, for example,
> *woman, desk, happiness, Andrew.*

la **abertura** opening
el **abismo** gulf
el **aburrimiento** boredom
el **abuso** abuse
el **acceso** access
la **acción** (*pl* acciones) action
el **acento** accent
el **ácido** acid
el **acontecimiento** event
la **actitud** attitude
la **actividad** activity
el **acuerdo** agreement; settlement
la **advertencia** warning
la **afirmación** (*pl* afirmaciones) claim
la **agencia** agency
la **agenda** diary
el/la **agente** agent
la **agitación** (*pl* agitaciones) stir
el **agujero** hole
la **alcantarilla** drain
la **alcayata** hook
la **alegría** joy
el **alfabeto** alphabet
el **alfiler** pin
el/la **aliado/a** ally
el **aliento** breath
el **alivio** relief
el **alma** (*f*) soul
el **almacén** (*pl* almacenes) store
el/la **amante** lover
la **ambición** (*pl* ambiciones) ambition
la **amenaza** threat
el/la **amigo(a)** mate

la **amistad** friendship
el **amor** love
el **análisis** (*pl inv*) analysis
la **anchura** breadth; width
el/la **anfitrión(ona)** host
el **ángel** angel
el **ángulo** angle
la **angustia** anguish
el **animal doméstico** pet
la **antigüedad** antique
el **anuncio** announcement
el **anzuelo** hook
el **apoyo** support
la **aprobación** (*pl* aprobaciones) approval
la **apuesta** bet; stake
la **armada** navy
el **arreglo** compromise
la **artesanía** craft
el **artículo** article; item
la **asociación** (*pl* asociaciones) association
el **asombro** astonishment
el **aspecto** aspect
la **astilla** splinter
el **asunto** affair
el **atajo** short-cut
el **ataúd** coffin
la **atención** (*pl* atenciones) attention
el **atentado** attempt
la **atracción; el atractivo** attraction
la **ausencia** absence
la **autoridad** authority

la aventura adventure; affair
el aviso notice
la ayuda assistance, help
el/la ayudante assistant
el ayuntamiento council
el azar chance
la bala bullet
la bañera tub
la barandilla rail
la barrera barrier
el barril barrel
la base base
la batalla battle
la batería battery
la beca grant
el beso kiss
la Biblia Bible
el/la blogero(a) blogger
la bolsa bag
la bomba bomb
la bondad kindness
el borde edge
la broma joke
el brote outbreak
el bullicio bustle
la burbuja bubble
el cable cable
la caja box
la calcomanía transfer
el cálculo calculation
el caldo stock
la calidad quality
la calma calm
el camino path; way
el campamento camp
la campaña campaign
el camping (*pl* ~s) site
el canal channel
el/la canguro baby-sitter

la cantidad amount
el caos chaos
la capa layer
la capacidad ability; capacity
el capítulo chapter
la característica characteristic; feature
la caridad charity
el cartucho de tinta ink cartridge
el/la catedrático(a) professor
el cazo pot
los celos jealousy (*sing*)
el centro centre; focus; middle
el centro turístico resort
la cesta basket
el chiste joke
el cielo heaven
la cima top
el círculo circle
las circunstancias circumstances
la cita quote; extract; appointment
el/la civil civilian
la civilización (*pl* civilizaciones) civilization
la clase sort; period
la clasificación (*pl* clasificaciones) classification
la codicia greed
la columna column
el columpio swing
la combinación (*pl* combinaciones) combination
el combustible fuel
el comentario comment, remark
el/la comentarista commentator
las comillas: entre comillas inverted commas: in quotes
la comisión (*pl* comisiones) commission

el **comité** (*pl* comités) committee
el **compañero** fellow
la **comparación** (*pl* comparaciones) comparison
la **compasión** (*pl* compasiones) sympathy
la **competición** (*pl* competiciones) contest
el/la **competidor(a)** rival
la **comprensión** (*pl* comprensiones) sympathy
el **compromiso** commitment
la **comunicación** (*pl* comunicaciones) communication
la **comunidad** community
la **concentración** (*pl* concentraciones) concentration
la **conciencia** conscience
la **condecoración** (*pl* condecoraciones) honour
la **condición** (*pl* condiciones) condition; status
la **conducta** conduct
la **conexión** (*pl* conexiones) connection
la **conferencia** conference
la **confianza** confidence
el **conflicto** conflict
el **confort** comfort
el **congreso** conference
la **conmoción** (*pl* conmociones) shock; disturbance
el **conocimiento** consciousness; knowledge
la **consecuencia** consequence
el **consejo** advice
la **construcción** (*pl* construcciones) construction; structure
el/la **consumidor(a)** consumer

el **contacto** contact
el **contenido** content
el **contexto** context
el **contorno** outline
el **contraste** contrast
la **contribución** (*pl* contribución) contribution
la **conversación** (*pl* conversaciones) conversation
la **copia** copy
el **corazón** (*pl* corazones) heart; core
la **corona** crown
el/la **corresponsal** correspondent
la **corrupción** (*pl* corrupciones) corruption
la **cortesía** politeness
la **cosa** thing
las **cosas** stuff (*sing*)
la **costumbre** custom
el **crecimiento** growth
el/la **criado(a)** servant
la **crisis** (*pl inv*) crisis
la **crítica** criticism
el **cuadro** picture
la **cuba** tub
el **cubierto** place
el **cuchicheo** whispering
la **cuenta** count
  por su **cuenta** of his own accord
el **cuento** tale
la **cuestión** (*pl* cuestiones) question
la **cueva** cave
el **cuidado** care
la **culpa** blame
la **cultura** culture
la **cuota** fee
la **curiosidad** curiosity
los **datos** data (*pl*)
el **debate** debate

el deber duty
la decepción (*pl* decepciones) disappointment
la decisión (*pl* decisiones) decision
el defecto fault
la definición (*pl* definiciones) definition
el/la dependiente(a) assistant
la depresión (*pl* depresiones) depression
el/la derecho(a) right
  los derechos fee
el desagüe drain
el desarrollo development
el desastre disaster
el descanso break
el/la desconocido(a) stranger
la desdicha unhappiness
el deseo desire; wish; urge
el desgarrón (*pl* desgarrones) tear
la desgracia misfortune
el desorden disorder; mess
el destino destiny; fate
la destreza skill
la destrucción (*pl* destrucciones) destruction
la desventaja disadvantage
el detalle detail
la devolución (*pl* devoluciones) refund; return
el diagrama diagram
el diálogo dialogue
la diana target
el diario diary; journal
la diferencia difference
la dificultad difficulty
la dimensión (*pl* dimensiones) dimension
el Dios God

el/la diplomático(a) diplomat
el/la diputado(a) deputy
la dirección (*pl* direcciones) direction
la disciplina discipline
el discurso speech
la discusión (*pl* discusiones) argument; discussion
el diseño design
el dispositivo device
la disputa dispute
la distancia distance
la división (*pl* divisiones) division
el drama drama
la duda doubt
el eco echo
la economía economics (*sing*); economy
la edición (*pl* ediciones) edition
el efecto effect
el ejemplar copy
el ejemplo example
  por ejemplo for instance
el/la elector(a) elector
la elegancia elegance
el elemento element
la encuesta survey
el/la enemigo(a) enemy
la energía energy
el entusiasmo enthusiasm; excitement
la envidia envy
la época period
el equilibrio balance
el equipo equipment
el error mistake
el escándalo scandal
el escape leak
la escasez shortage
la escritura writing

el **esfuerzo** effort
el **espacio** space
la **espalda** back
la **especie** species (*sing*)
el **espectáculo** show; sight
la **esperanza** hope
el **espesor; la espesura** thickness
el **esquema** outline; diagram
la **estaca** stake
la **estancia** stay
la **estatua** statue
el **estilo** style
la **estrategia** strategy
el **estrés** stress
la **estructura** structure
el **estudio** studio
la **estupidez** (*pl* estupideces)
  stupidity
la **etapa** stage
la **excepción** (*pl* excepciones)
  exception
el **exceso** excess
la **excusa** excuse
el/la **exiliado(a)** exile
el **exilio** exile
las **existencias** stock
el **éxito** success
la **experiencia** experience
el/la **experto(a)** expert
la **explicación** (*pl* explicaciones)
  explanation
la **explosión** (*pl* explosiones)
  explosion
  una **explosión** a bomb blast
las **exportaciones** exports
la **exposición** (*pl* exposiciones)
  exhibition
la **expresión** (*pl* expresiones)
  expression

la **extensión** (*pl* extensiones) extent
el **extracto** extract
el/la **extranjero(a)** foreigner
la **fabricación** (*pl* fabricaciones)
  manufacture
la **facilidad** facility
el **factor** factor
el **fallo** failure
la **falta:** absence
  falta (de) lack (of)
la **fama** reputation
el **favor** favour
la **fe** faith
la **felicidad** happiness
la **fila** row
la **filosofía** philosophy
el **fin** end
la **flecha** arrow
el **fondo** background; bottom; fund
el/la **forastero(a)** stranger
la **forma** form; shape
la **fortuna** fortune
el **fracaso** failure
la **frase** sentence; phrase
la **frente** front
el **frescor, la frescura** freshness
la **fuente** source
la **fuerza** force; strength
la **función** (*pl* funciones) function
la **ganancia** gain
el **gancho** hook
los **gastos** expenses
la **generación** (*pl* generaciones)
  generation
el **gol** goal
el **golfo** gulf
el **golpe** bang; blow; knock
la **gotera** leak
el **grado** degree

el gráfico chart
el grito cry
el grupo group
la guía guide
el hambre (*f*) hunger
el hecho fact
la higiene hygiene
la hilera row
el honor honour
los honorarios fee
la honra honour
el hueco gap
el humo fumes (*pl*); smoke
el humor humour
la idea idea
  no tengo ni idea I haven't a clue
el idioma language
el/la idiota fool; idiot
la imagen (*pl* imágenes) image
la imaginación (*pl* imaginaciones) imagination
el impacto impact
el imperio empire
las importaciones imports
la importancia importance
la impresión (*pl* impresiones) impression
el impuesto duty
el impulso urge
la inauguración (*pl* inauguraciones) opening
el incidente incident
la independencia independence
el índice index
la indirecta hint
la infancia childhood
el infierno hell
la influencia influence
los ingresos earnings

el/la inspector(a) inspector
el instante instant
la institución (*pl* instituciones) institution
el instituto institute
las instrucciones instructions
el instrumento instrument
la intención (*pl* intenciones) intention; aim
el interés (*pl* intereses) interest
el/la internauta internet user
la interrupción (*pl* interrupciones) interruption
el intervalo gap
la investigación (*pl* investigaciones) research
la invitación (*pl* invitaciones) invitation
la ira anger
el jaleo row
el/la jefe(a) chief
el juego gambling
los juegos del ordenador gaming
el juguete toy
la lágrima tear
la lata can
el/la lector(a) reader
la leyenda legend; caption
la libertad freedom
la licenciatura degree
el/la líder leader
la liga league
el límite boundary; limit
la limpieza cleanliness
la línea line
la liquidación (*pl* liquidaciones) settlement
la lista list
la literatura literature

el **local** premises (*pl*)
la **locura** madness
el **logro** achievement
la **loncha** slice
la **longitud** length
el **lugar** site
el **lujo** luxury
la **luz** (*pl* luces) light
  luz de la luna moonlight
el/la **maestro(a)** master
la **magia** magic
la **manera** manner
la **máquina** machine
la **marca** brand; mark
el **marco** frame
el **margen** (*pl* márgenes) margin
la **máscara** mask
la **matrícula** fee
el **máximo** maximum
la **mayoría** majority
el **medio (de)** means (of)
la **mejora, la mejoría** improvement
la **memoria** memory
la **mente** mind
el **método** method
la **mezcla** mixture
el **miedo** fear
el **milagro** miracle
la **mina** mine
el **mínimo** minimum
el **ministerio** ministry
la **minoría** minority
la **mirada** glance
la **misa** mass
la **misión** (*pl* misiones) mission
el **misterio** mystery
el **mitin** (*pl* mítines) rally
el **mito** myth
la **moda** fashion; trend

la **molestia** annoyance
el **molino** mill
el **montón** (*pl* montones) mass; pile
la **moral** morals (*pl*)
el **mordisco** bite
el **motivo** pattern
el **motor** motor
el **muchacho** lad
la **muchedumbre** crowd
la **muestra** sample
la **muñeca** doll
la **naturaleza** nature
el **naufragio** wreckage (*sing*)
la **negociación** (*pl* negociaciones)
  negotiation
el **nervio** nerve
la **niñez** childhood
el **nivel** level
el **nombramiento** appointment
la **nota** note
el **número** number; issue
la **objeción** (*pl* objeciones) objection
el **objetivo** objective; purpose;
  target
el **objeto** object; goal
las **obras** works
el **odio** hate
el/la **oficial** officer
la **olla** pot
el **olor** smell
la **opción** (*pl* opciones) option
la **opinión** (*pl* opiniones) opinion
la **oportunidad** chance; opportunity
la **oposición** (*pl* oposiciones)
  opposition
la **orden** (*pl* órdenes) order
la **organización** (*pl* organizaciones)
  organization
organización benéfica charity

el orgullo pride
el origen (*pl* orígenes) origin
la oscuridad darkness
la paciencia patience
la página page
la paja straw
la palabra word
el palacio palace
el palo stick
el pánico panic
el paquete pack; packet
el paquete de programas software
  package
la pareja pair
la parte part
  parte de arriba top; **parte
  delantera** front; **parte trasera** rear;
  de parte de algn on behalf of sb
la partida item
el parto labour
  estar de parto to be in labour
el pasaje; el pasillo passage
la pasión (*pl* pasiones) passion
el paso footstep
el patrón (*pl* patrones) pattern
la pausa pause
el pedazo piece
el pedido order
el peligro danger
la pena distress; penalty
el penalty (*pl* penalties) penalty
el pensamiento thought
el periódico journal
el periodo period
el/la perito(a) expert
el permiso permission
la persona person
el personal personnel
la perspectiva prospect

la pesadilla nightmare
la picadura bite
la pieza piece; item
la pila battery; pile
la pista clue
el placer delight; pleasure
el plan plan; scheme
el plato dish
la plaza place
el poder power
el poema poem
la política politics (*sing*); policy
la póliza policy
el polvo dust
la pompa bubble
el porcentaje percentage
la porción (*pl* porciones) portion
el portavoz (*pl* portavoces)
  spokesman
la posibilidad possibility
la posición (*pl* posiciones) position
el post post (*on forum or blog*)
la práctica practice
la preferencia choice
el prefijo code
la pregunta question
el premio award
la preparación (*pl* preparaciones)
  preparation
los preparativos arrangements
la presencia presence
la presión (*pl* presiones) pressure
el presupuesto budget; quote
la princesa princess
el príncipe prince
el principio beginning; principle
la prioridad priority
el problema problem; trouble
el proceso process

el/la profesor(a) master
la profundidad depth
el programa schedule
la prohibición (*pl* prohibiciones) ban
el propósito purpose
  a propósito on purpose
la propuesta proposal
la prosperidad prosperity
la protección (*pl* protecciones)
  protection
la protesta protest
las provisiones provisions
el proyecto plan
la publicidad publicity
la puja bid
la punta point
la puntería aim
el punto item; point
  punto de partida starting point;
  punto de vista point of view
el/la querido(a) darling
la rabia rage
la raja crack
el rato while
la razón (*pl* razones) reason
la reacción (*pl* reacciones) reaction;
  response
la realidad reality
la rebanada slice
el/la rebelde rebel
el recado message
la recepción (*pl* recepciones)
  reception
la recesión (*pl* recesiones) recession
la reclamación (*pl* reclamaciones)
  claim
el recuerdo souvenir
el recurso resource
  como último recurso as a last resort

la red network
la reducción (*pl* reducciones)
  reduction
la reforma reform
la regla period
la reina queen
la relación (*pl* relaciones) relationship
la religión (*pl* religiones) religion
la reputación (*pl* reputaciones) status
el requisito requirement
la reserva fund; stock
la resistencia resistance
la resolución (*pl* resoluciones)
  resolution
el respecto: con respecto a with
  regard to
el respeto respect
la respiración (*pl* respiraciones) breath
la responsabilidad responsibility
la respuesta reply; response
los restos remains; wreckage (*sing*)
el resultado outcome
el reto challenge
el retrato portrait
la reunión (*pl* reuniones) meeting
la revista magazine; journal
el rey (*pl* ~es) king
el riel rail
el ritmo pace
el/la rival rival
la rodaja slice
el ruido noise
la ruina ruin
el rumor rumour
la ruptura break
la rutina routine
el sacrificio sacrifice
el/la santo(a) saint
la sección (*pl* secciones) section

el **secreto** secret
el **sector** sector
la **sed** thirst
la **seguridad** security; safety
la **selección** (*pl* selecciones)
 selection; choice
el **sentido** sense; way
el **sentimiento** feeling
la **señal** sign; mark
el **señor** lord
el **servicio** service
la **sesión** (*pl* sesiones) session
el **significado** meaning
el **silbato** whistle
el **silencio** silence
el **símbolo** symbol
el **sindicato** trade union
el **sistema** system
el **sitio** place
la **situación** (*pl* situaciones) situation
el/la **socio(a)** member
la **soledad** loneliness
la **solución** (*pl* soluciones) solution
la **sombra** shadow
el **sondeo (de opinión)** poll
el **sonido** sound
el **soporte (físico)** hardware
la **sorpresa** surprise
la **sospecha** suspicion
la **subasta** auction
el **subtítulo** caption
la **subvención** (*pl* subvenciones)
 grant
la **suciedad** dirtiness
el **sueño** sleep
la **suerte** luck
  buena/mala suerte good/bad luck
la **sugerencia** suggestion
el **suicidio** suicide

la **suma** sum
la **superficie** surface
la **supervisión** (*pl* supervisiones)
 supervision
el/la **superviviente** survivor
el/la **suplente** substitute
el **surtido** choice
la **sustancia** substance
el/la **sustituto(a)** substitute
la **táctica** tactics (*pl*)
el **talento** talent
la **tapa** top
la **tapicería, el tapiz** (*pl* tapices)
 tapestry
el **tapón** (*pl* tapones) top
la **tarea** task
la **tarifa; la tasa** rate
el **teatro** theatre; drama
la **técnica** technique
la **tecnología** technology
el **tema** theme; issue
la **tendencia** trend
la **tensión** (*pl* tensiones) tension;
 strain
la **tentativa** attempt; bid
la **teoría** theory
el **territorio** territory
el **terrón** (*pl* terrones) lump
el **texto** text
la **tienda** store
la **timidez** shyness
el **tipo** type; kind; fellow, guy
el **tío** (*Sp*) guy
la **tirada** edition
el **título** title
el **tomo** volume
la **tortura** torture
el **total** total
la **tradición** (*pl* tradiciones)

tradition
la trampa trap
la tranquilidad calmness
la transferencia transfer
el tratamiento treatment
el trato deal; treatment
la tristeza sadness
el trozo bit; piece; slice
el truco trick
el tubo tube
la tumba grave
el tumor growth
el turno turn
la unidad unit
la valentía bravery, courage
el valor value
el vapor steam
la variedad variety; range
la vela candle

el veneno poison
la ventaja advantage; asset
la verdad truth
la vergüenza shame
la versión (*pl* versiones) version
la victoria victory
la vida life
el vínculo bond
la violencia violence
la visita; visit; visitor
el/la visitante visitor
la vista sight
el volumen (*pl* volúmenes) volume
el/la voluntario(a) volunteer
el/la votante voter
la vuelta turn; return
  dar una vuelta to go for a stroll;
  dar una vuelta en bicicleta to go
  for a bike ride

VERBS

> **What is a verb?**
> A **verb** is a 'doing' word which describes what someone or something does, what someone or something is, or what happens to them, for example, *be*, *sing*, *live*.

abandonar to abandon
abrigar(se) to shelter
abrir to turn on
  abrir(se) to open
abrochar to fasten
aburrir to bore
  aburrirse to get bored
acabar de hacer algo to have just done sth
acampar to camp
aceptar to accept
acercarse (a) to approach
  acercarse a to go towards
aclarar(se) to clear
acompañar to accompany; to go with
aconsejar to advise; to suggest
acordarse de to remember
acostarse to lie down
acostumbrarse a algo/algn to get used to sth/sb
actuar to act; to operate
acusar to accuse
adaptar to adapt
adelantar to go forward; to overtake
adivinar to guess
admirar to admire
admitir to admit
adoptar to adopt
adorar to adore
adquirir to acquire; to purchase
afectar to affect
afirmar to assert; to state

agarrar to catch; to grab; to grasp
agradecer to thank (for)
aguantar to bear
ahorrar to save
ahuyentar to chase (off)
alcanzar to reach
  alcanzar a algn to catch up with sb;
  alcanzar a ver to catch sight of
alimentar to nourish
aliviar to relieve
almacenar to store
alojarse to put up
  alojarse con to lodge with
alquilar to hire; to rent: to let
amar to love
amenazar to threaten
amontonar to stack
andar to walk
anhelar to long for
animar to encourage
  animar a algn a hacer algo to urge sb to do sth
anunciar to advertise; to announce
añadir to add
apagar to switch off; to turn off; to put out
apagar to turn off
  apagarse to fade
aparecer to appear
apetecer to fancy
  me apetece un helado I fancy an ice cream

aplastar to crush
aplaudir to applaud; to cheer; to clap
aplazar to postpone; to put back
aplicar a to apply to
apostar (a) to bet (on)
apoyar to support; to endorse
  apoyar(se) to lean
apreciar to appreciate
aprender to learn
apretar to press; to squeeze
aprobar to approve of; to endorse
aprovechar to take advantage (of)
apuntar to take down
arañar to scratch
arrancar to pull out
arrastrar to drag
  arrastrarse to crawl
arreglar to fix (up); to arrange; to settle
  arreglárselas to cope; to manage
arrepentirse de to regret
arriesgar to risk
arrojar to hurl
arruinar to ruin
asar to bake
ascender to promote
asegurar to assure; to ensure;
  to secure
asentir con la cabeza to nod
asfixiar(se) to suffocate
asistir (a) to attend
asombrar to amaze; to astonish
asustar to alarm; to frighten;
  to startle
atacar to attack
atar to attach; to tie
atender to treat
  atender a to attend to
atraer to attract
atrasar to hold up

atreverse (a hacer algo) to dare
  (to do sth)
aumentar to increase; to raise
avanzar to advance
averiarse to break down
averiguar to check
avisar to warn
ayudar to help
azotar to whip
bailar to dance
bajar: to come down; to go down;
  to lower
  bajar (de): to get off; **bajar de** to
  get out of
balbucir to stammer
barrer to sweep
basar algo en to base sth on
batir to whip; to beat
besar to kiss
bombardear to bomb
brillar to shine; to sparkle
bromear to joke
burlarse de to make fun of
buscar to look for; to search; to seek
caerse to fall (down)
  se me cayó I dropped it
calcular to estimate
calentar(se) to heat (up)
callarse to be quiet
cambiar to alter; to exchange
  cambiar(se) to change
cancelar to cancel
cantar to sing
capturar to capture
carecer de to lack
cargar (de) to load (with)
causar to cause
cavar to dig
celebrar to celebrate

centellear to sparkle
cerrar: to turn off: to close; to fasten
  cerrar(se): to shut; **cerrar con**
  llave to lock
charlar to chat
chillar to scream
chismear to gossip
chocar con to bump into
chupar to suck
citar to quote
clasificarse to qualify
cobrar to claim; to get
coger to catch; to grab; to seize
colaborar to collaborate
coleccionar to collect
colgar to hang (up)
colocar to place
combinar to combine
comenzar (a) to start (to)
cometer to commit
compaginar to combine
comparar to compare
compartir to share
compensar to compensate (for)
  compensar por to make up for
competir en to compete in
complacer to please
completar to complete; to make up
comprar (a) to buy (from)
comprender to comprise
comunicar to communicate
conceder to grant
concentrarse to concentrate
concertar to arrange
concluir to conclude; to accomplish
condenar to condemn; to sentence
conducir to lead
conectar to connect
confesar to confess

confiar to trust
  confiar en to rely on
confirmar to confirm
confundir (con) to confuse (with)
  confundir a algn con to mistake
  sb for
congelar to freeze
conocer to know
conseguir to achieve; to get; to secure
  conseguir (hacer) to succeed (in
  doing)
considerar to consider; to rate
constar de to consist of
  hacer constar to record
constituir to constitute; to make up
construir to build; to put up
consultar to consult
consumir to consume
contar to count
  contar con to depend on
contemplar to contemplate
contener to contain; to hold
contestar to answer
continuar to continue; to keep;
  to resume
contribuir to contribute
controlar to control
convencer to convince
convenir to suit
convertir to convert
copiar to copy
correr to run
cortar to cut (off); to mow
costar to cost
crear to create
crecer to grow
creer to believe; to reckon
criar to bring up
criticar to criticize

cruzar to cross
cubrir (de) to cover (with)
cuchichear to whisper
cuidar to look after; to take care of;
to mind
 cuidar de to take care of
cultivar to cultivate
cumplir to accomplish; to carry out
curar to heal
dañar to harm
dar to give:
 dar a to overlook; dar asco a to
 disgust; dar de comer a to feed;
 dar la bienvenida to welcome;
 dar marcha atrás to reverse;
 dar saltitos to hop; dar un paseo
 to go for a stroll; dar un puñetazo a
 to punch; dar una bofetada a to
 slap; dar vergüenza a to embarrass;
 dar vuelta a to turn; darse cuenta
 de algo to become aware of sth;
 darse por vencido to give up;
 darse prisa to hurry;
deber must; to owe
 deber hacer algo to be supposed
 to do sth; debo hacerlo I must do it
decepcionar to disappoint
decidir(se) (a) to decide (to)
decidirse (a) to make up one's mind
(to)
decir to say; to tell
declarar to declare
 declarar culpable to convict;
 declararse en huelga to (go on)
 strike
decorar to decorate
dedicar to devote
defender to defend
definir to define

dejar to leave
 dejar caer to drop
deletrear to spell
demorar(se) to delay
demostrar to demonstrate
depender de to depend on
derribar to demolish
desanimar to discourage
desaparecer to disappear
desarrollar(se) to develop
descansar to rest
descargar to unload
describir to describe
descubrir to discover; to find out
desear to desire; to wish
deshacerse de to get rid of
deslizar(se) to slip
desnudarse to strip
despedir to dismiss
despegar to take off
despejar(se) to clear
despertar(se) to wake up
desprenderse to come off
desteñirse to fade
destruir to smash
desviar to divert
detener to arrest
determinar to determine
detestar to detest
devolver to bring back; to give back;
to send back
 devolver a su sitio to put back
dibujar to draw
diferenciarse (de) to differ (from)
dimitir to resign
dirigir to conduct; to direct; to
manage
disculparse (de) to apologise (for)
discutir to argue; to debate; to discuss

diseñar to design
disfrazar to disguise
disfrutar to enjoy
disminuir to decline; to decrease;
  to diminish
distinguir to distinguish
distribuir to distribute
divertir to divert
  divertirse to enjoy oneself
dividir to divide; to split
doblar to fold
  doblar(se) to double
dominar to dominate; to master
ducharse to shower
dudar to doubt
durar to last
echar to pour:
  echar a algn to throw sb out;
  echar a algn la culpa de algo
  to blame sb for sth; **echar al correo**
  to post; **echar de menos** to miss;
  echar una mirada a algo to glance
  at sth; **echarse** to lie; **echarse a**
  llorar to burst into tears; **echarse**
  a reír to burst out laughing
educar to bring up; to educate
ejecutar to execute
elegir to choose; to select; to elect
elogiar to praise
emocionar to excite
empatar to draw, to tie
empezar (a) to begin (to)
emplear to employ
empujar to push
encarcelar to imprison
encender to switch on; to turn on;
  to light
encerrar to shut in
encontrar to find; to meet

enfocar to focus
enjugar to wipe
enseñar to teach; to show
entender to understand
enterarse de to hear about
enterrar to bury
entrar (en) to enter
entregarse to give oneself up;
  to surrender
entrevistar to interview
enviar to send
envolver to wrap up
equivocarse to make a mistake;
  to be mistaken
erigir to erect
escapar (de) to escape (from)
escarbar to dig
escoger to choose; to pick
esconderse to hide
escuchar to listen (to)
especializarse en to specialize in
especular to gamble
esperar to wait (for); to expect;
  to hope
establecer to establish; to set up
  establecerse to settle
estallar to blow up
estar to be
  estar acostumbrado a algo/
  algn to be used to sth/sb; **estar de**
  acuerdo to agree; **estar de pie** to
  be standing; **estar dispuesto a**
  hacer algo to be prepared to do
  sth; to be willing to do sth;
  estar equivocado to be wrong;
  estar involucrado en algo to be
  involved in sth
estirar(se) to stretch (out)
estrecharse la mano to shake hands

estrellar(se) to crash
estropear to ruin
estropear(se) to spoil
estudiar to study; to investigate
evitar (hacer) to avoid (doing)
exagerar to exaggerate
examinar to examine
examinarse to sit an exam
excitar to excite
exclamar to exclaim
excluir to exclude; to suspend
existir to exist
experimentar to experience
explicar to explain
explorar to explore
explotar to explode
exponer to display
exportar to export
expresar to express
exprimir to squeeze
expulsar temporalmente to suspend
extender to spread: to extend
extender(se) to spread out
extrañar (*LAm*) to miss
fabricar to manufacture
faltar to be lacking; to fail
felicitar to congratulate
fiarse de to trust
financiar to finance
fingir to pretend (to)
firmar to sign
flotar to float
fluir to flow
formar(se) to form
forzar a algn a hacer (algo) to force sb to do (sth)
fotografiar to photograph
frecuentar to frequent
freír to fry

funcionar to work
(hacer) funcionar to operate
fustigar to whip
ganar to earn; to gain
garantizar to guarantee
gastar to spend: to waste
gastar(se) to wear (out)
gemir to groan
golpear to knock; to beat
grabar to record
gritar to shout; to scream; to cry
guardar to keep; to store
guiar to guide
gustar to like
haber to have
hablar to speak; to talk
hacer to do; to make; to bake
hacer añicos to shatter; **hacer campaña** to campaign; **hacer comentarios** to comment; **hacer daño a** to hurt; **hacer las maletas** to pack; **hacer preguntas** to ask questions; **hacer público** to issue; **hacer señas** *or* **una señal** to signal; **hacer una lista de** to list; **hacer una oferta** to bid; **hacer una pausa** to pause; **hacer una señal con la mano** to wave; **hacerse** to become; to get; **hacerse adulto** to grow up; **hacer(se) pedazos** to smash
helarse to freeze
herir to injure
hervir to boil
huir to flee; to run away *or* off
identificar to identify
iluminar(se) to light
imaginar to imagine
impedir to prevent (from)

implicar to imply; to involve
imponer to impose
importar to matter; to mind; to care
  ¡no me importa! I don't care!;
  ¿y a quién le importa? who cares?
impresionar to impress
imprimir to print
inclinar to bend
  inclinarse to bend down
incluir to include
indicar to point out; to indicate
influir to influence
informar to inform
inscribirse to register
insinuar to hint
insinuar to imply
insistir en to insist on
instruir to educate
insultar to insult
intentar to attempt to
interesar to interest
  interesarse por to be interested in
interrogar to question
interrumpir to interrupt
introducir to introduce
invadir to invade
investigar to investigate
invitar to invite
  invitar a algn a algo to treat sb to sth
ir to go
  ir a buscar a algn to fetch sb;
  ir bien a to suit; **ir deprisa** to dash;
  ir en bicicleta to ride a bike
irse to go away
irritar to irritate; to aggravate
jugar to play; to gamble
juntarse con to join
jurar to swear
justificar to justify

juzgar to judge
lamentarse to moan
lamer to lick
lanzar to throw; to launch
  lanzarse a to rush into
leer to read
levantar to raise; to put up; to lift
  levantarse to get up; to rise
limpiar to clean
llamar to call
  llamar por teléfono: to ring;
  llamarse to be called
llegar to arrive
llenar (de) to fill (with)
llevar: to carry; to bear; to wear
  llevar a cabo to carry out;
  llevarse to take
llorar to cry, weep
llover to rain
  llover a cántaros to pour
luchar to fight; to struggle
maltratar to abuse
manchar to dirty
mandar to command, to order
manifestarse to demonstrate
mantener to maintain; to support
  mantener el equilibrio to balance
marcharse to depart; to leave
medir to measure
mejorar(se) to improve
mencionar to mention
mentir to lie
merecer to deserve
meterse en to get into
mezclar to mix
mimar to spoil
mirar to look (at); to watch
  mirar fijamente to stare at
modificar to adjust

molestar to annoy; to disturb; to trouble

montar a caballo to ride

morder to bite

morir to die

mostrar to hold up
  mostrar(se) to show

mover to move

multiplicar to multiply

nacer to be born

necesitar to need

negar to deny
  negarse (a) to refuse (to)

negociar to negotiate

notar to note

obedecer to obey

obligar a algn a to oblige sb to

observar to notice; to observe

obstruir to block

obtener to obtain

ocasionar to bring about

ocultar to hide

ocupar to occupy
  ocuparse de to deal with

ocurrir to occur

odiar to hate

ofender to offend

ofrecer to offer
  ofrecerse a hacer algo to volunteer to do sth

oír to hear

oler to smell

olvidar to forget

operar a algn to operate on sb

oponerse a to oppose; to object to

organizar(se) to organize

otorgar to award

pagar to pay

pararse to come to a halt, to stop

parecer to seem (to); to look
  parecerse a to look like, to resemble

participar en to take part in

partir to share
  partir(se) to split

pasar to pass; to overtake; to spend

pedir to request; to order
  pedir a algn que haga algo to ask sb to do sth; **pedir algo a algn** to ask sb for sth; **pedir algo prestado a algn** to borrow sth from sb

pegar to hit; to stick; to strike

pensar to think
  pensar en to think about; **pensar hacer** to intend to do

perder to miss:
  perder a algn de vista to lose sight of sb

perdonar a to forgive

perdurar to survive

permitir to allow, to permit, to let
  permitirse to afford

perseguir to pursue

persuadir to persuade

pertenecer a to belong to

pesar to weigh

picar to bite

pinchar(se) to burst

planchar to iron

plegar to fold

poder to be able to; can; might
  ¿puedo llamar por teléfono?: can I use your phone?; **el profesor podría venir ahora:** the teacher might come now; **puede que venga más tarde** he might come later

poner to put; to lay
  poner de relieve to highlight; **poner en duda** to question; **poner**

en el suelo to put down; **poner en orden** to tidy; **ponerse** to put on; **ponerse de pie** to stand up; **ponerse en contacto con** to contact
portarse to behave
poseer to own, to possess
practicar to practise
precipitarse to rush
predecir to predict
preferir to prefer
preguntar (por) to inquire (about)
  preguntarse to wonder
prender fuego to catch fire
preocupar to trouble; to bother
  preocuparse (por) to worry (about)
preparar(se) to prepare
prescindir de to do without
presentar to present; to introduce
prestar to lend
prevenir to warn
prever to foresee
privar to deprive
probar to prove
producir to produce
prohibir to ban; to forbid
prometer to promise
pronosticar to predict
pronunciar to pronounce
propagarse to spread
proponer to propose
proteger to protect
protestar to protest
proveer to provide
publicar to publish
quedar to remain
  quedarse to stay
quejarse (de) to complain (about)
quemar to burn

querer to want (to); to love; to like
quitar to remove
  quitar algo a algn to take sth from sb; **quitarse** to take off
reaccionar to react; to respond
realizar to fulfil; to realize
reanudar to resume
recalcar to emphasize; to stress
rechazar to reject
recibir to receive
  recibirse (*LAm*) to qualify
reclamar to demand; to claim
recoger to pick (up); to collect; to gather
recomendar to recommend
reconocer to recognize
recordar to recall
  recordarle a algn to remind sb of
recuperarse to recover
reducir(se) to reduce
reembolsar to refund
referirse a to refer (to)
  en lo que se refiere a ... as regards ...
reflejar, reflexionar to reflect
reformar to reform
regañar to tell off
regar to water
registrar to register; to examine
reír to laugh
  reírse de to laugh at
relajarse to relax
relatar to report
renovar to renew
reñir to quarrel
reparar to repair, to mend
repartir to deal; to deliver
repetir(se) to repeat
reponer to replace
  reponerse to mend

representar to perform; to represent
requerir to require
resbalar to slide
reservar to book; to reserve
resistir to hold out
  resistir(se) to resist
resolver to solve
respetar to respect
respirar to breathe
responder to reply, to answer;
  to respond
restaurar to restore
resultar to prove
retar to challenge
retirar(se) to withdraw
reunir(se) to collect
  reunirse to gather; **reunirse con**
  to rejoin
revelar to reveal
rodear (de) to surround (with)
romper(se) to break; to tear;
  to burst
ruborizarse to blush
saber a to taste of
saber to know
  sé nadar I can swim
sacar to bring out; to take out
  sacar brillo to polish; **sacarse el**
  título to qualify
sacudir to shake
salir to emerge
saltar to leap
saludar to greet
  saludar con la cabeza to nod
salvar to rescue; to save
secar(se) to dry
seguir to follow
  seguir haciendo algo to go on
  doing sth

sentarse to sit (down)
sentir to be sorry
  sentir(se) to feel
señalizar to indicate
ser to be
servir to serve
significar to mean
sobrevivir to survive
solicitar to apply to; to seek
soltar to release
sonar to sound
  (hacer) sonar to ring
sonreír to smile
sorprender to surprise
sospechar to suspect
subir to climb; to come up; to go up
  subir a to board; to get on
suceder to happen
sufrir (de) to suffer (from)
  sufrir un colapso to collapse
sugerir to suggest
sujetar to fix
suministrar to supply
suponer to assume; to suppose;
  to involve
surgir to emerge
suspender to suspend; to fail
suspirar to sigh
sustituir to replace
telefonear to telephone
temblar to shake
temer to fear
tender to hold out
tener to have; to hold
  tener antipatía a to dislike; **tener**
  cuidado to be careful; **tener éxito**
  to be successful; **tener lugar**
  to take place; to come off; **tener**
  mala suerte to be unlucky; **tener**

miedo to be afraid; **tener que** to have to; **tener que ver con** to concern; **tener razón** to be right; **tener suerte** to be lucky; **tener tendencia a hacer algo** to tend to do sth
terminar to end; to finish
tirar to throw away
  tirar de to pull
tocar to touch; to play; to ring
tomar to take
torcer to twist
trabajar to work
traducir to translate
traer to bring
traicionar to betray
tranquilizar(se) to calm down
trasladar to transfer
tratar to treat
  tratar (de) to try (to); **tratar con** to deal with
unir to join
  unir(se) to unite

untar to spread
usar to use
vaciar(se) to empty
vacilar to hesitate
valer to be worth
variar to vary
vencer to conquer, to defeat, to overcome
vender to stock
  vender(se) to sell
venir to come
  venirse abajo to collapse
ver to see
visitar to visit
vislumbrar to catch sight of
vivir to live
volar to fly
volcar to overturn
volver to come back; to go back; to return
  volver(se) to turn round; **volverse hacia** to turn towards
votar to vote

ENGLISH
INDEX

The words on the following pages cover all of the ESSENTIAL
and IMPORTANT NOUNS in the book.

absence 71
accident 40, 112, 134
Accident and Emergency
  113
accommodation 122
account 131
actor 170
actress 171
address 121, 129
adults 78
advert(s) 98
aerobics 166
afternoon 175
age 63, 78
agriculture 61
air 58, 74, 198
air pollution 181, 183
airbed 30, 157
airport 10
airsickness 12
alarm clock 124, 174
alcohol 88
alphabet 66
Alps 106
aluminium 138
ambition 33
ambulance 113
America 53
American 54, 55
Andalusia 106
animal(s) 14, 74, 82
ankle 22
anorak 44
answer 69
answerphone 130
antiseptic 112
apartment 120
aperitif 88
appearance 62
apple 101
appliance 102
application 35
appointment 29, 113
apprenticeship 34, 66
apricot 100

April 26
area 75, 199
arm 22
armchair 102
armed robber 134, 135
army 134
arrival 11, 187
art gallery 96, 180
article 162
ashtray 95, 124
aspirin 113
Atlantic 106
atmosphere 170
attachment 131
audience 170
auditorium 170, 171
August 26
aunt 79
au pair girl 81
author 34
autumn 26, 198
avenue 121
baby 78
bachelor 80
back 23, 195
bag 10, 44, 187
baker 163
bakery 161
balcony 116, 120
Balearic Islands 106
ball 166, 167, 169
ballet 170
banana 100
band 142
bandage 113
bank 32, 128, 160, 180
bank account 131
bank card 129
banknote 128, 160
bar 88, 116
barbecue 31
Barcelona 106
barrier 189
basement 120
basketball 166

Basque Country 106
bath 125
bathroom 116, 118, 120,
  202
bathtub 119
battery 41
Bay of Biscay 106
beach 75, 157
bean 192
beard 63
beauty 65
bed 103, 113, 203
bed linen 127, 203
bedroom 120
bee 153
beef 89
beer 89
beginning of term 66
Belgian 55
Belgium 53
belt 44
bench 152, 180
bicycle 19, 187, 195
bidet 126
bike 19, 187, 195
bikini 156
bikini bottoms 44
bill 89, 117, 119
billboard 173
billiards 166
biofuel 74
biology 67
bird 14, 15, 20
Biro® 128
birth 28
birthday 28
blackboard 69
blanket 125
block of flats 120, 180
blood 23, 113
blouse 45
boarding card 11
boat 156, 157, 194
body 22
bodywork 41

bonfire 29
book 68
bookcase 103
booking 173
bookshop 163
boot 40, 45
border 41, 189
boss 32, 33, 34
bottle(s) 75, 89
bottom 156
boutique 163, 181
bowl 88
box 31, 89
box office 171
boxer shorts 44
boy 78
boyfriend 98
bracelet 151
brake 18, 38, 186
branch 153, 191
brand 163
bread 90
break 68
breakdown 41
breakdown van 41
breakfast 88, 116, 202
breathalyzer® test 41
brick 138
bridge 58, 180, 186
Britain 53
British girl/woman 55
Briton 54, 55
broadband 131
brother 78
brush 124, 150
Brussels 106
budgie 20
building 120, 180
bunch of flowers 152
bunk bed 203
burglar 134, 135
burglary 134
bus 180, 194
bus station 181
bus stop 181

bush 152
business 34
businessman/woman 34, 35
bust 22
butane store 30
butcher 163
butcher's (shop) 161
butter 89
button 44
café 88, 180
cafeteria 91
cage 15
cake 91
cake shop 89, 161
calculator 163
calendar 27
calf 14, 82
call 129
callbox 131
camcorder 99
camera 97
camp bed 31
camper 30, 31
campfire 31
camping 30
campsite 30
can 30, 31, 88, 89
Canada 52
Canadian 54, 55
Canary Islands 106
cancellation 11
canned food 89
canteen 67
capital (city) 107
car 38, 74, 180, 194
carbon footprint 75
car door 41
car hire 10
car park 38, 120, 180
car wash 40
carafe 91
caravan 31, 38, 39, 195
cardboard 138
cards 97

career 35
careers adviser 32, 33
caretaker 34, 35, 122, 123
carpet 125
carriage 186
carrot 193
cart 194
cartoon 98
cash desk 161
cast 172
Castile 106
castle 58, 182
cat 14, 15, 82
Catalonia 106
cathedral 181
cauliflower 193
CD 96, 98
CD/DVD player 96, 102
CD/DVD writer 99
cellar 121
cent 160
central heating 120
century 174
cereal 88
certificate 70
chain 151
chair 103
chairperson 34, 35
chambermaid 119
champion 166, 167
championship 166
change 116, 128, 160
character 64
chauffeur 38, 39
check-out 129, 161
check-out assistant 32, 33
checkpoint 134
cheek 23
cheese 90
chef 91, 92
chemist 32, 112, 113
chemist's (shop) 113, 161
chemistry 69
cheque 116, 128, 160
cheque book 130, 160

cherry 101
chess 96, 166
chest 22, 103
chestnut 101
chicken 90
child 78, 79
child benefit 80
chimney 123
chin 23
chips 89
chocolate 88
choice 91
Christian name 78
church 183
cider 88, 91
cigar 95
cigarette 95
cinema 96, 170, 171, 180
circus 170
city 121, 181
civil guard 60, 61, 134, 135
clarinet 142
class 67, 187
classical music 97
classroom 67
cleaner 35, 123, 127
climate 74, 198
climate change 74
clinic 113
clock 12, 102, 174
clothes 45
cloud 199
clown 170, 171
club 66, 96
clutch 40
coach 194
coast 75, 157
coat 14, 44
cobbler 162
cock 20, 82
coffee 88, 180
coffee pot/maker 125
coffee table 103
coffee with milk 88
Coke® 89

cold 112, 198
collar 44
colleague 34, 35
collection 99, 131
collision 40, 41
colour 62
comb 150
comedian 170, 171
comedy 173
comfort 117, 121
comic strip 97
compact disc 98
compartment 186
competition 98
competitive exam 71
complaint 119, 163
complexion 65
comprehensive school 66
computer 50, 51, 68
computer programmer
  32, 33
computer science 51
computer studies 67
concert 66, 96
condition 138
conductor 142, 143
confectioner 163
congratulations 108
connection 10, 186, 187
consulate 134
contact lenses 65
contract 34
cook 35, 88
cooker 103, 125, 126
cooking 203
cordial 92
cordless phone 102
corkscrew 30
corner 181
corridor 70, 122
Corunna 106
Costa del Sol 106
costume 44, 170
cottage 123
cotton 138

cotton wool 112
couchette 189
council flat 181
counter 128
counter clerk 128, 129
country 52, 58, 74, 82
country people 61
countryman 58, 82
countryside 58
countrywoman 59, 83
course 90, 166
court 166, 167
cousin 78, 79
cover charge 92
covering letter 35
cow 15, 83
crab 86, 156
cream 91, 113
credit 130
credit card 129, 161
cricket 166
crisis 75
crisps 89, 91
croissant 88
crop 152
crossing 157
crossroads 38, 182
culprit 134, 135
cultivation 152
cup 91
cupboard 102, 122, 124
curiosity 65
curtain(s) 125, 171
customer 160, 161
customs 11, 187
customs officer 10, 11, 186,
  187
cycling 18, 166
cyclist 18, 38, 39
daddy 78
damage 40, 74, 134
dance 96
dashboard 40
date 29, 117
daughter 79

day 27, 66, 174, 175
day off 70
days of the week 27
dead man/woman 134, 135
death 29, 135
death penalty 135
debit card 129, 161
December 26
deckchair 31, 157
decorator 34
defence 169
degree 198
delay 10, 176, 186
demonstration 135
dentist 112, 113
deodorant 150
department 160, 161
department store 160
departure 11, 187
departure gate 11
departure lounge 13
deposit 116, 128
desk 102
dessert 90
dessertspoon 91
destination 12, 188
detective novel 97
detergent 74
dialling code 128
dialling tone 128
diarrhoea 113
diesel 38, 74, 138
diesel oil 38
digital camera 99
digital radio 103
dining car 188
dining hall 66
dining room 120, 202
dinner 89
diploma 70
direction 39, 187
director 170, 173
directory 129
disco 97
discount 160

dish 90
dishes 91, 125
dishwasher 102, 126
display case 163
distance 39, 195
district 59, 180
diversion 39, 183
divorce 28
DIY 178
doctor 32, 33, 112, 113
dog 14, 15, 82
door 41, 121
dormitory 66, 202
double bed 117
draught beer 91
drawing 66
dress 44
dress circle 170
drink 89
drive 121
driver 38, 39, 188, 189
driving licence 38, 39
driving school 41
drug 112
drum kit 143
drums 143
dry-cleaner's 163
duck 20, 82
duration 13
dust 60, 126, 200
dustbin 30, 124, 202
Dutchman 54
Dutchwoman, Dutch girl
  55
duty-free (shop) 11
DVD 96
ear 23
earth 59, 75, 83
east 106, 198
eau de toilette 151
e-book 70, 102
ecology 75
Edinburgh 106
editor 32, 33
education 67

egg 88
electric cooker 103
electrician 32
electricity 125
electronics 67
elephant 14
email 128, 130
emergency exit 11
employee 32, 33
employer 32
employment organisation
  34
engagement 28
engine 40
engineer 32
England 53
English 66
Englishman 54
Englishwoman, English
  girl 55
enquiries 129
entertainment 97
entrance 11, 117, 121, 187
entrance examination 71
envelope 128
environment 74
environmentalist 74
era 177
e-reader 102
escalator 13, 163, 189
estate 61
e-ticket 12
euro 128, 160
euro cent 128
Europe 53
European 54, 55
evening 99, 175
ewe 15, 83
exam 66
exchange 66
exchange rate 130
exercise book 66
exhaust fumes 74
exhibition 99
exit 11, 171, 187

expense 130
experiment 66
expression 65
exterior 120
extra charge 30, 92, 130, 186
eye 22, 62
eyebrow 23
fabric 138, 139
face 22, 23
face cream 151
factory 33, 75, 181
fair 29
fair trade 92, 162
family 79
fare 10, 11, 186, 189, 194
farm 59, 83
farmer 32, 33, 58, 59, 60, 61, 82, 83
farmer's wife 83
farmhouse 59, 83
fashion 45
fast train 186
father 78
father-in-law 80
fault 135
fax 128
fax machine 128
February 26
fence 59, 83, 153
ferry 194
festival 28, 29
festivities 29
fiancé 78
fiancée 79
field 58, 82, 166, 167
file 70, 71
film 97, 98, 171
film star 97, 171
fine 135
finger 22
fire 134
fire engine 194
fire escape 117
fireman 32, 34

fireplace 123
firework; firework display 28
first course 90
first name 78
fish 14, 74, 86, 90
fish shop 89
fisherman/woman 156, 157
fishing 167
fishing boat 156
fishmonger 163
fishmonger's 161
fixed price menu 90
fixed term contract 34
flat 120
flavour 92
flea market 162
flight 12
flight attendant 32, 33
floor 116, 117, 120, 121
flour 91
flower shop 161
flower(s) 75, 153
flowerbed 153
flu 113
flute 143
fly 87
foal 14
fog 199
folder 71
food 161
foot 22
football 166
forecast 198, 201
forehead 23
forest 58, 75, 82
fork 30, 90
form 116, 117, 128
fortnight 175
foyer 172
France 53
free time 96
freezer 102
French 66

French beans 192, 193
French loaf 89
Frenchman 54
Frenchwoman, French girl 55
Friday 26
fridge 102, 124, 125
front 195
front door 121
fruit 75, 89, 101
fruit juice 90
fruit tree 100
fruiterer 163
fruiterer's 161
frying pan 127
full board 117
fun fair 28
fur 14, 139
furnished flat 122
furniture 102, 120, 122
future 34, 176
future tense 176
game 96, 166, 167
games console 97
games room 31, 203
gang 135
garage 38, 39, 120
garage owner 32, 38
garden 120, 152
gardener 152, 153
gardening 153
garlic 92, 192
gas 30, 74, 124, 138
gas cooker 103
gate 59, 83, 153
gear 19, 41
geography 67
German 54, 55, 66
Germany 53
girl 79
girlfriend 99
glass 74, 90, 138
glasses 63
glove 44
goal 166, 167

goalkeeper 168
gold 138
goldfish 86
golf 166
goose 20
government 74, 134
grandchildren 80
granddaughter 81
grandfather 78
grandmother 79
grandparents 78
grandson 80
grant-aided school 70
grape(s) 101
grapefruit 100
grass 153
Great Britain 53
green salad 193
greengrocer 162, 163
greengrocer's 161
greenhouse 82
Greens 74
grilled meat 91
grocer's 161
ground 58, 59, 83, 153
ground floor/level 117, 121
group 66
grown-ups 79
guest 116, 117
guest house 117, 119
guidebook 119, 203
guitar 143
gym 66, 67
gymnast 166, 167
gymnastics 167
habit 65
hair 14, 22, 62
hairdresser 34, 35, 163
half an hour 175
half-board 117
hall 31
ham 88
hamburger 89
hamster 14
hand 23

hand luggage 10
handbag 44, 129, 135, 163, 186, 187
handicrafts 68
handkerchief 44
handyman/woman 178, 179
harbour 156
hard-boiled egg 88
hat 44
head 23
headlight(s) 38, 40
headmaster 66
headmistress 67
health 113
heart 22
heat 74, 198
heater 102, 103, 127
heating 121
heavy goods vehicle 194
height 63
helicopter 12, 194
helmet 18, 194
hen 21, 83
higher school-leaving course/certificate 70
high-speed train 186
highway code 40
hike 59, 97, 203
hill 61, 83
history 67
hitch-hiker 38, 39
hitch-hiking 38
hoarding 173
hobby 96, 97
hockey 166
hold-up 134
hole 74
holiday-maker 156, 157
holidays 69, 203
Holland 53
home address 130
homework 66, 69
hood 45
horizon 156

horn 40
hors d'oeuvres 88
horse 14, 82
horse-racing 169
horse-riding 167
hospital 112
hot chocolate 88
hotel 116, 180
hour 175
house 121
housework 125
housing 123
housing estate 121
hunger 89
hunter 58, 59
husband 78, 80
hypermarket 160
ice 198
ice cream 88
ID 63
ID card 10, 128, 134
identity 135
identity card 135
identity theft 137
illness 113
inclusive price 92, 118
income tax 134
industrial estate 183
information 11, 129, 187
information desk 11
inhabitant(s) 74, 180, 181
injection 113
injury 113
inn 60, 61, 118
insect 86
institute of employment 34
instrument 142
insurance 40, 112
insurance certificate 39
insurance policy 41, 135
interior 120
internet 96
internet café 130, 172
interval 170

interview 35
Ireland 53
Irishman 54
Irishwoman, Irish girl 55
iron 103, 138
island 75, 157
Italian 54, 66
Italy 53
jacket 45
jam 89
January 26
jeans 44
jersey 168
jewel 150
job 32, 34
job centre 35
job interview 35
job market 34
journey 38, 186
jug 91
July 26
jumper 44
June 26
jungle 75
kettle 102
key 117, 121, 179
kid 82
kilometre 38
kitchen 121, 203
kitten 14
knee 23
knickers 44, 45
knife 30, 88
knitting 98
laboratory 68
lady 79
lake 60, 74
lamb 14, 82, 92
lamp 18, 103, 125
lampshade 103
land 59, 153
landing 122
landline 130
landlord/lady 122, 123
languages 67

laptop 102
launderette 31, 181
laundry 127
lawn 122
lawyer 134, 135
leading lady 173
leading man 170
leaf 61, 153, 191
leaflet 96
leather 138, 139
lecture 71
left luggage locker/office 187
leg 23
leisure (activities) 98
lemon 100
lemonade 89
length (of time) 189
length 13
lesson(s) 67
letter 129
letterbox 124
library 35, 163, 183
life 33
lift 116, 120
light 125
light bulb 127
lighter 95
lilo® 157
line 187
lion 14
list 161
listings section 173
litre 38
living room 120, 121
lock 127
locker 187
London 106
look 65
lorry 38, 194
lorry driver 40
lost property office 131, 187
luggage 10, 116, 186
lumber room 122
lunch 88, 89, 116, 117

machine 179
magazine 97
maiden name 78
mail 130
main road 39
main street 183
Majorca 106
make (of car) 41
make-up 150, 172
Malaga 106
man 78
manager 34, 35, 116, 117, 163
map 12, 68, 74, 186, 202
March 26
mare 83
marina 156
mark 69
market 58, 160, 180
marmalade 89
marriage 28
match 30, 31, 95, 166, 168
mathematics, maths 67
May 26
mayonnaise 91
mayor 182, 183
meal 89, 117, 203
means of transport 194
meat 89
mechanic 32, 38
medicine 112, 113
Mediterranean 106
meeting 99
melon 100
member 96
membership card 202
menu 89
metal 138
microwave oven 102
milk 89
milky coffee 88
miner 32
mineral water 88
Minorca 106
minute 174

mirror 30, 102, 124, 150
mist 201
mistake 66, 128
mixed salad 89
mobile phone 96, 102, 130
mock exam 66
(modern) languages 67
moment 174
Monday 26
money 160
month 27, 174
monument 182
mood 64
moped 194
morning 175
mosque 183
mother 79
mother-in-law 81
motorbike 195
motorcycle 195
motorcyclist 40, 41
motorhome 31
motorist 40, 41
motorway 39
MOT test 41
mountain 59, 75
mountain bike 19
mountain range 106
mouse 14, 50
moustache 62
mouth 23
move 123
MP3 player 102
mugger 134, 135
mugging 134
multiple-journey ticket 183
mummy 79
museum 96, 180
mushrooms 192
music 69, 97, 143, 171
music video 170
musical instrument 142
musician 142, 143
mustard 91
mutton 92

name 78
napkin 125
nationality 55
nature 64
neck 22
neighbour 80, 81, 122, 123
nephew 80
Netherlands 52
news 97, 98
news stand 182
newsagent 163
newspaper 74, 96
next day 176
niece 81
night 31, 117, 175, 203
nightdress 44
noise 58, 116
north 106, 198
(Northern) Ireland 53
nose 23
notebook 66
notice 98, 170, 182
novel 97
November 26
nuclear plant 75
number 10, 38, 116, 128, 186
nurse 32, 33, 112, 113
nursery school 67
oar 156
October 26
office 33, 70, 181, 203
official papers 40
oil 38, 88
ointment 113
old town 183
olive 89
omelette 91
one-way street 41
onion 193
opera 171
operation 113
operator 130, 131
optician 34
oral exam 70

orange 101
orchestra 143, 171
outing 67, 97
oven 126
overcoat 44
owner 88, 122, 123, 134, 135
ox 14, 82
pain 112
paint 127
painter 34, 35
painting 99, 103, 127
Pakistani 54, 55
pal 66, 67
pancake 91
pants 44, 45
paper 70, 138
papers 135
parasol 201
parcel 128
parents 78
park 180, 182
parka 45
parking 40
parking meter 182
parking space 120, 121, 180
Pakistani 54
parrot 20
party 29, 97
passenger 10, 11
passer-by 182, 183
passport 10, 116, 128, 186
past 176
past tense 176
pastry 89
pâté 90
path 58, 152
patient 112, 113
pavement 183
payment 130
PC 50, 98, 99
PE 67
peace 61
peach 100
pear 101
peas 192, 193

pedestrian 38, 180
pedestrian precinct 183
pen 129
pen friend 96, 97
pencil 68
pencil case 70
penknife 31
people 79
pepper 91, 192
performance 171
perfume 150
perfume
shop/department 161
permanent contract 34
permission 134
person 63, 79
personal computer 50,
 98, 99
personal stereo 96
pétanque 169
petrol 39, 75
petrol pump 40
petrol pump attendant
 40
petrol station 39, 181, 183
phone call 131
phonecard 131
phone company 129
phone contract 128
phone number 120
photo 97, 125
physics 67
piano 102, 142
picnic 58, 90, 156
picture 102, 124
piece of fruit 89
piece of furniture 102, 120
pig 14, 82
pill 113
pillow 125
pilot 12, 13, 34
pineapple 101
pipe 95
pitch 30, 166, 167
pity 110

pizza 91
place 182
place setting 92
plane 10, 194
plane crash 12
plane ticket 10
planet 75
plant(s) 75, 153
plaster cast 113
plastic 138
plate 30, 90
platform 186
play 166, 171
player 166, 167
playground 70
playtime 68
plot of land 120, 121
plug 126
plumber 34
pocket 44
pocket money 96
police 39, 135, 181
police officer 182, 183
police station 135, 181
policeman 32, 38, 134, 180
policewoman 135, 181
politics 35
pollutant 74
pollution 75
pop music 97
pork 88
pork butcher 163
pork butcher's 161
pork chop 91
port 156
porter 116, 186
post office 129, 161, 181
postbox 128
postcard 129
postcode 128
poster 98, 124, 170, 182
postman 32, 128
postwoman 33, 129
potato 193
pound (sterling) 129

power steering 39
practical class 67
prescription 113
present 28, 160, 176
present tense 176
presentation 67
president 34, 35
press 97
price 116, 128, 160
price list 203
primary school 67
primary schoolteacher 67,
 68
printer 51
private hospital 113
private school 70
prize 68
problem 134
profession 33
program 50
programme 96, 98, 170
programmer 50
progress 68
property 61
public holiday 27
public transport 194
publicity 97
puncture 18, 40
pupil 66, 67
puppy 14
purchase 161
purse 130, 134, 163
pyjamas 44
Pyrenees 106
quality 65
quarter 88
quarter of an hour 174
quay 156
question 69, 75
quiche 90
rabbit 14, 92
race 169
radiator 124
radio 97, 103, 125
radio alarm 102

railway 188
rain 75, 153, 199
rain forest 191
raincoat 44
rainfall 201
raisin 101
raspberry 101
rate(s) 117, 203
razor 151
reading 67, 97
ready-made meals 89
receipt 118, 186
reception 117
receptionist 33, 116, 117
recipe 91, 127
record 96
recorder 143
reduction 161, 186
region 75, 199
registration document 39
relative 78
rent 122
reply 129
report 71, 135
reservation 11, 187
restaurant 90, 92, 116, 180
restricted parking zone 41, 183
result 68, 166
retirement 33
return ticket 10, 186
review 173
reward 131, 135
rice 88
right of way 41
ring 150
rise 34
river 58, 74
road 39, 59, 181, 183
road accident 40
road map 38
road surface 61
roadblock 134
roast 88
roast chicken 90

robber 134, 135
rock 59
Rock (of Gibraltar) 106
roof 122
room 31, 103, 117, 121
root 153
rope 179
rose 153
roundabout 41
rowing 156
rowing boat 194
rubber 67, 138
rucksack 31, 203
rug 125
rugby 166
rule 71
ruler 71
rules 31, 71, 203
sail 167
sailing 167
sailing boat/ship 194
saint's day 28
salad 89, 193
salami 90
sales 161
sales assistant 32, 33, 160, 161
salesman/woman 160, 161
salt 89
sand 157
sandal 45
sandcastle 156
sandwich 90
Saragossa 106
sardine 87
Saturday 26
saucepan 124, 125
saucer 90
sausage 89
saxophone 142
scales 125
scenery 58
school 66, 67
school friend 66, 67
schoolboy 66

schoolgirl 67
science 67
scooter 195
Scot 54, 55
Scotland 53
sea 74, 156
seafood 86, 90
seasickness 156
seaside 157
season 27, 199
season ticket 182
seat 170, 173, 186
seat belt 12, 40
second 174
secondary school 66
secretary 33
self-service restaurant 88, 90
semester 68
sentence 67
September 26
serial 99, 172
service 90
set price 92
Seville 106
shade; shadow 31, 153
shampoo 150
sheep 83
sheepdog 82
sheet 125, 203
shelf 103
ship 156
shirt 45
shoe 44
shoe shop 161
shoe size 44, 160
shop 161, 181
shop assistant 32, 33, 160, 161
shop keeper 34, 163
shop window 163
shopping centre 160
shorts 44
shoulder 22
show 96, 170

shower 31, 117, 121, 125, 200, 203
showing 171
sideboard 102
signature 129
silence 202
silk 139
silver 139
SIM card 131
singer 96, 97
singing 96
single ticket 10, 186
single woman 81
sink 124
sister 79
site 30
situation 34
size 44, 45, 63, 160, 161
skating rink 97
ski 166
ski slope 169
skiing 166
skin 23, 101
skirt 45
skittles 168
sky 20, 198
sleeping bag 30, 202
sleeping car 188
slice 89
slipper 45
slot 131
slum area 180
small ads 98
smell 92
smile 65
smoke 122, 200
snack 92
snails 92
snow 199
soap 99, 124
sock 44
socket 30, 31, 126
sofa 102
soft-boiled egg 88
soil 58, 59, 153

soldier 32
solution 75
son 78
song 97
soundtrack 171
soup 88, 91
south 106, 198
South America 53
souvenir 160
sow 83
Spain 53
Spaniard 54, 55
Spanish 66
Spanish railway 189
spanner 179
spare part 41
spare tyre 41
special offer 163
species 75
speed 13, 19, 41
speed camera 38
spoon 31, 89
spoonful 113
sport 166
spot 64
spring 26, 199
spy 134, 135
square 181
stadium 166
staffroom 69
stage manager 172
stainless steel 138
stairs 117, 121
stalls 170, 173
stamp 128, 131
star 33, 97, 172, 173
starter(s) 88, 90
state school 70
station 181, 187
station buffet 187
stay 117, 203
steak 88
steel 138
stepfather/mother 80, 81

stereo system 102
steward 32, 33
sticking plaster 112
stomach 22, 112
stone 59, 139, 157
storey 116, 117, 120, 121
storm 201
story 67
stove 30
strawberry 101
stream 58
street 121, 181
street map 38
stretcher 113
strike 35
student 66, 67
studies 51, 66
study (of) 66
subject 67
subtitle 172
suburb 180
subway 180, 186, 194
sugar 88
suit 44
suitcase 11, 117, 187
summer 26, 198
summer holidays 69
sun 152, 198
sunburn 113, 157
suncream 157
Sunday 26
sunglasses 156, 157
sunny spell 200
sunset 201
sunshine 198
supermarket 160
surgery 113
surname 78
surroundings 180
sweets 88
swimmer 156, 157
swimming 69, 157, 167
swimming pool 31, 67, 69, 117, 167, 181
swimming trunks 44, 156

swimsuit 44, 156
swine flu 113
Swiss 54, 55
Swiss girl, Swiss woman 55
switch 118, 124
Switzerland 53
synagogue 183
synthetic fibre 138
syrup 92, 112
table 31, 89, 103
table football 96
tablespoon 91
tablet 103, 112, 113
tail 15
tap 124, 179
tape 99
tape recorder 67, 102
tart 91
task 69
taste 92
tax 74, 130
taxi 10, 180, 186, 194
taxi driver 32
taxi rank 181, 187
tea 90
teacher 32, 33, 68, 69
teaching 67
team 166
teapot 91
tear 63
teaspoon 91
teenager 80, 81
telegram 130
telephone 102, 116, 128
telephone directory 131
television 97, 103, 117, 125
television set 124
temp 34, 35
temperature 75, 113, 199
temping agency 35
temporary contract 34
tennis 166
tennis court 167
tent 31

text message 98, 128, 130
Thames 106
theatre 96, 170, 180
theft 134
thief 134, 135
thirst 91
throat 23
thumb 22
thunderstorm 201
Thursday 26
ticket 10, 96, 170, 171, 186
ticket collector 188, 189
ticket machine 183
ticket office 186, 187
tie 45
tiger 14
tights 45
time 74, 174, 175
timetable 10, 66, 186
tin 30, 31, 88, 89
tinned food 31
tin-opener 30
tip 91, 119, 173, 189
title 172
toast 91
tobacco 95
tobacconist's 95, 160
today's special 90
toilet 122, 124, 202
toilets 10, 30, 116, 202
toll 38
toll motorway 39
tomato 100, 192
tongue 23
tool 179
tooth 22
toothbrush 150
toothpaste 125, 151
top (of hill) 61
top-up card 131
torch 31
tortoise 15
tour 180
Tour of Spain 19

tourist 10, 11, 58, 59, 180, 181
tourist information office 129
towel 125, 157
tower 59, 181
town 121, 181
town centre 180
town council 180
town hall 180
toy 98
track 58, 167, 187
tractor 82
trade 32
trade union 34
traffic 40, 182, 183
traffic jam 38, 40, 182
traffic lights 38, 182
trailer 30
train 186, 194
train driver 32
train station 181
transistor 102
translation 71
travel agent's 10, 11, 161
traveller 10, 11, 186, 187
traveller's cheque 130
tray 89, 125
tree(s) 58, 74, 190
trip 10, 67, 97, 203
trolley 12, 92
trousers 44
trout 87
truck 38
truth 135
T-shirt 45
Tuesday 26
tumble-dryer 103
turkey 20, 82
TV 97
TV channel 97
twin beds 117
typist 33
tyre 18, 38, 41
ugliness 65

umbrella 44, 198
uncle 78
underground 180, 186, 194
underground station 187
underwear 45
unemployed person 34
unemployment 34
uniform 44
United Kingdom 52
United States 52
university 69
unleaded petrol 39
upkeep 122
USA 52, 53
usher 170
usherette 173
vacuum cleaner 103, 127
valley 58
van 59, 83, 195
vanilla 91
veal 91
vegetables 75, 91, 153, 193
vehicle 30, 194
video cassette 99
video game 96
video recorder 98, 102, 124
view 117, 121, 181
village 58, 82, 120
vinegar 90
violin 142
visibility 201
visitor 202, 203
voice 23, 65
voicemail 130
volleyball 166
wage-earner 34, 35
wages 32
waist 44, 62
waiter 88, 90, 92, 116
waiting room 187

waitress 91, 117
Wales 53
walk 58, 96, 156, 166
walking stick 58
wall 121
wallet 129, 135, 163, 187
warden 30
wardrobe 102, 124
washbasin 30, 118, 122, 124, 202
washing 127
washing facilities 31
washing machine 31, 103, 125
washing powder 30, 74, 126
washing-up liquid 126
washrooms 30
wasp 153
watch 150, 174
water 31, 39, 75, 87, 125, 157
water skiing 166
way 58
weather 74, 198
weather forecast 199, 201
weather report 198
web designer 32
website 98
wedding 29
wedding anniversary 28
Wednesday 26
weeds 153
week 27, 175
weekend 96, 174
welcome 119
wellington boot 61
Welshman 54
Welshwoman, Welsh girl 55

west 106, 198
western 170
wheel 19
widow 81
widower 80
wife 79, 81
wind 198
wind farm 74
wind turbine 74
window 121
windsurfing board 157, 167
wine 90
winter 26, 198
wireless 51
witness 134, 135
woman 79
wood 58, 74, 139, 190
wool 139
word 69
work 32, 68
worker 34, 35
working life 33
workshop 178
world 74
wound 113
writing paper 130
written exam 70
written proof 128
wrought iron 138
yard 120
year 67, 174
yoghurt 90
young man 78
young people 78
youth 78, 79
youth club 99
youth hostel 58, 202
zone 75
zoo 14, 182